# COMBAT READY

# COMBAT READY

## THE MAKING OF A FIGHTER PILOT

## DAVID MASON

BLOOMSBURY

First published in Great Britain 1991

Copyright © David Mason 1991

The moral right of the author has been asserted

Bloomsbury Publishing Ltd, 2 Soho Square, London W1V 5DE

A CIP catalogue record for this book
is available from the British Library

ISBN 0 7475 0259 5

10 9 8 7 6 5 4 3 2 1

Photoset by Rowland Phototypesetting Ltd,
Bury St Edmunds, Suffolk

Printed and bound in Great Britain by
Butler and Tanner Ltd, Frome and London

The pilot of a modern fighter aircraft has one of the most exhilarating and exacting jobs in the world. It is also one of the most coveted, and every year thousands of keen, hopeful, even desperate young men apply for training. For the young aspirant the route to qualification is supremely challenging, and few make it into a profession that remains difficult and dangerous. The fighter pilot may be barely out of his teens, yet he is equipped to go out, often entirely alone, in an aircraft that has cost up to £20 million, loaded with enough weapons to start World War III.

Few have any real idea of what life in the high-tech cockpit is really like. David Mason has done what millions have only dreamed of. Uniquely for a civilian, he has followed the entire selection and training process, from the first interview at Biggin Hill to flying a Tornado. (His prowess in the back seat of a Hawk trainer moved the instructor to observe that he was wasted as a journalist!)

*Combat Ready* is the perfect book for all armchair aviation enthusiasts; more than that, it offers to everyone a rare glimpse of the working lives of the heirs of the Few – from streaking through the Welsh hills at treetop height to air combat manoeuvres at 30,000 feet.

# Contents

# List of Illustrations

# INTRODUCTION

Half a century ago, in the air battles of the summer of 1940, young Allied fighter pilots were routinely sent into combat with no more than a handful of flying hours in their log-books. Those were desperate times, and the emergency demanded shortcuts and drastic solutions. Even so, the training of the combat pilot reflected the stage of development which his profession had reached, and the level of the technology which he was expected to understand and command.

Today, such has been the advance in the technology of aerial warfare, it takes between three-and-a-half and four years to bring a fighter pilot up to the level where he can go to war. Today's training is almost as long as the war itself was fifty years ago. And it takes that long not to become a fully proficient fighter pilot, but merely to achieve a basic grounding in the necessary skills. A simple catalogue of the subjects covered in the fighter pilot's training shows how extensive his range of competence must be.

The student pilot must first learn to fly, starting in simple propeller-driven aircraft, and advancing progressively to supersonic jets. He must master aerobatics, learning to link individual manoeuvres together in an elegant and efficient sequence. He must learn to fly on instruments, without reference to the world outside the cockpit. He has to learn to navigate, at height and at low level, and to do so both visually and without reference to the outside world, relying entirely on his instruments. He needs to be able to fly at night, and has to be able to manoeuvre his aircraft in close formation with other aircraft. He has to understand the technology of his aircraft and its systems. And he has to cover all these sub-disciplines on each of the aircraft types that he flies in successive stages of his training.

After all that, he goes on to study and master the skills of aerial combat, both at low level and at height, and to apply them alongside other aircraft in a formation, sometimes acting as their leader. And he has to learn to lead a formation when it is 'bounced' by 'enemy' aircraft.

Having mastered those flying skills, he goes into the third stage of his training, and learns to operate the specific weapons system in which he will serve on his squadron. That alone, in the modern fighter aircraft, represents a suite of advanced technologies which will tax the learning capacity of all but the most agile and receptive mind.

Even to begin all that, and certainly in order to be allowed to continue his training, the student pilot must demonstrate a level of health and fitness which is virtually faultless. He must also pass through the selection and training processes for activities which are designed solely to prove his suitability as an officer, and have nothing whatever to do with flying.

Evidently, not everybody can meet every requirement in all these categories. But some of them are indispensable, and it is interesting to try to define what qualities a young person needs if he (and now she) is to survive the selection and training process.

It was to try to find some of the answers to those questions that I set out to write this book. The book's origin can be traced back to one morning some time ago, when I was a passenger in a Hawk advanced trainer. The Royal Air Force instructor who was flying the aircraft let me take control, and after a few minutes he casually remarked that I might have made the grade as a fighter pilot. Perhaps he was joking, and in any case I had reached the age where such remarks are harmless and largely irrelevant. Nevertheless his observations set me wondering exactly what qualities it took for ordinary young men to pass through the succeeding hurdles on the way first to wings standard, and from there to a position on a front-line squadron. Today, the world of military flying is also open to women. When the Royal Air Force first surprised the aviation community by accepting women student pilots, the plan was not to offer them combat assignments, and they would therefore not be selected for advanced jet training. They would normally be streamed at the end of the basic course into the multi-engined sector, with prospects of working in transport, air-to-air refuelling, or airborne surveillance. There is, however, a potential flaw in that plan. If a female student were to prove especially successful in basic training, it would be difficult to deny her her chance on fast jets. Then, if she emerged among the best students on that course, there is one area where she could be employed in fast jets – as a 'creamed off' instructor on that same advanced course, in the Hawk aircraft. Even if she cannot yet train for combat, the female student is not entirely barred from the exciting world of fast-jet flying.

As the research for the book progressed, it became obvious that few people have the slightest idea what combat pilots do for a living. Most have a hazy idea that they control an aircraft with a stick and a throttle, and zoom about the sky downing enemy aircraft with machine-guns. Some, notably those who have some connection with aviation, know that training to fly modern combat aircraft is difficult and challenging, and that a great many candidates are 'chopped' in the course of the training. Beyond that, the trade of the fighter pilot, and the training for it, is a complete mystery to the outside world. Yet large numbers of young people, some of them suitable, some demonstrably unsuitable, have an insatiable yearning to become fighter pilots. Many are certain to be disappointed.

As I contemplated these questions, I decided that it would be fascinating to find out something about the way the modern fighter pilot is selected and trained, and that if I were interested in the question, then other people who were also not fighter pilots might enjoy sharing that information. So this book was born.

Fortunately, the Royal Air Force also saw some value in letting the world know about the business of training to fly fighters. It would be unkind to suggest that the Royal Air Force has a vested interest, hoping the more that is known about the job the more young people of the right quality might want to try it. Equally, it could be said that a book like this might put people off the idea. After all, from selection, through every stage of training, and even on the squadron, life for the student pilot is difficult, physically and intellectually demanding, and potentially humiliating, since every candidate risks failure at any time in the course, and especially at the periodic and frequent test stages. Being chopped, when your friends and fellow students seem to be progressing effortlessly towards the goal that you shared with them, can be bitterly disappointing and only the most thick-skinned candidate could shrug off the humiliation.

Nevertheless, despite the risks inherent in letting me loose among their students, the Royal Air Force proved enthusiastic supporters of the idea of the book, and offered every facility that I asked for. Most notably they welcomed me at the relevant flying school for every stage in the course, and allowed me to fly every aircraft in the training inventory, from the two primary trainers, to the two most modern fighters in the armoury, at the advanced training units where pre-squadron pilots learn to operate the complete weapons system.

Nor was that support confined to the upper ranks of the service, whose authority I needed to get the book off the ground. In the course of visiting the Royal Air Force's training schools, some of them more than once, I talked with dozens of students, instructors, and other officers of all ranks. All of them gave me the benefits of their hard-won knowledge with unfailing enthusiasm, willingness and courtesy. So, perhaps, as one senior officer suggested, they should, but the fact that they all did so, without exception, remains the strongest recollection of my time spent researching this book – except, of course, for the flying.

It would be impossible to thank individually all the Royal Air Force personnel who gave their time and knowledge, but I would like to thank those who gave even more, and flew me, and even submitted to being flown by me, in their aircraft. Those QFIs (qualified flying instructors) spend their working days teaching people how to fly, but their normal students are at least competent in all the skills up to the one being dealt with on the day. In me they had a 'student' who had not gone through the course to that point, so they had to make some curious leaps through the syllabus, and they had to suffer some peculiar flying from an over-age and under-qualified visitor in the student seat. They remained polite, or at least kept their reactions to themselves, and I hope it will not be a blot on their careers if I publicly thank those whose names now appear in my flying log-book under the title 'Captain': Fl Lt Drew, Sq Ldr Braithwaite, Sq Ldr Hudson, Fl Lt Frost, Sq Ldr Thurley, Sq Ldr Dummer, Fl Lt Pearson, and Fl Lt MacDonald. And, although I never managed to fly with him, Wing Commander Stannard, who was especially patient and helpful with information on the introduction of the new Tucano aircraft.

# INTRODUCTION

Above all I should like to thank Air Commodore (as he then was) 'Sandy' Hunter, whose personal commitment and enthusiasm as Director of RAF Public Relations led to the germ of an idea being converted into a viable project. His successor Mike Barnes maintained the essential support, and he and his staff at both Support Command and Strike Command have my gratitude.

It is impossible in a single book to cover every aspect of a training programme that lasts for up to four years, and it would be unwise to try to do so without ploughing comprehensively through the course itself. Since it takes two or more flying manuals to cover each segment of the syllabus, obviously the complete course cannot be covered in a single book, and I have not attempted to do that. What I have tried to do is give a flavour of the kind of pleasures, excitements, targets, and obstacles that lie ahead for the young person who chooses to take up this career. I hope I have been able to convey the fact that it is enormously gratifying, uniquely challenging and, above all, incomparably exciting. I also hope I have been able to reveal something of those qualities that it takes to become one of the small number of fighter pilots. If I had to summarise the essential attributes, by way of an introduction to this book, I would say that it needs a good level of basic intelligence; a relish for flying (of the more exuberant military variety) that refuses to be denied and just about amounts to a passion; a determination to get through the course however hard the going; and a range of sub-skills such as co-ordination, mechanical sympathy, topographical instinct, and capacity to stay calm and think clearly under the most extreme pressures. On the other side of the equation, it would be reasonable to summarise the benefits. This is not a job for someone who wants to become a millionaire: you cannot expect to get rich from life in the services. But it is a demanding job for somebody who wants to be spared the boredom of a lifetime commuting into town; who hates being deskbound; and who looks forward to a career with a generous slice of adventure and excitement attached to it. Not that I would want to portray the average Royal Air Force combat fight pilot as an irresponsible adventurer. Indeed they all come across as extremely reasonable people. I was struck during the course of these researches by the difference between Royal Air Force officers I met and those I had encountered in other air forces. Fighter pilots in some nations (and I know that these are considerable generalisations) come across as natural streetfighters. The Royal Air Force's front-line officers seem a more gentlemanly breed, self-assured and cheerful, but undemonstrative – the kind of young men who, if they had taken a different route, might have joined the ranks of the city accountancy firm, or the teaching profession, or even, perhaps, the clergy.

That presents something of a paradox, when it is recalled that in this service, the officers are the front-line troops. It is they who go to war. Other ranks provide the back-up, in contrast to other services where, again in general terms, the front line is manned by junior ranks, who are commanded by officers. That fact itself raises one other concern. Apart from training for the hugely enjoyable work of flying aircraft, these young men are training for the distinctly unenjoyable task of going to war. It is not a prospect that they relish: I found no gung-ho militarism among them. But they are aware of the possibility of being ordered into combat, and were quite prepared to take it on as their responsibility should the time come when they are asked to put their training into practice.

Overall, Royal Air Force trainee fighter pilots seemed to me to be motivated by two things. One is the desire, the enthusiasm, and the determination to fly as Royal Air Force fighter pilots, and to enjoy doing so. The other is the sense of duty that drives them to do their best, to achieve, and to succeed – for themselves, for their fellow pilots in the schools and in the squadrons, and for the service.

I hope I have been able to convey that unique mix of qualities. Above all, I hope I have succeeded in showing that the life of a military pilot is a profession. It is, even, in its distinctive fashion, that rarest of combinations in these relatively dull modern times: a profession with a touch of spice.

D.M.

# 1

## Delta Hotel at Donna Nook

The speed is 420 knots – nearly 500 mph. The height is 250 ft, low enough to see the people in the farms and villages below, and to count the legs on the sheep. The weather, for once, is kind, with fine spring sunshine and a layer of haze on the horizon. I can carry out a visual attack. Behind me in the rear cockpit the navigator, who is also known as the weapons systems operator, is punching buttons in response to my requests, reporting into my headphones as each stage in the operation is completed, helping to set up the aircraft for the attack.

To the east the coastline is visible in the haze. We have been flying for more than an hour on this sortie, from our base in East Anglia, north and then west across to the other side of the country, into the border counties of Scotland, then back across the Pennines and the moorlands of Yorkshire, over the rich farmland of Lincolnshire, and finally back into East Anglia, mostly at low level.

Fuel is down to 240 kg. We have enough for one pass at the target, then we shall have to return to base. The aircraft is purring away like a quality automobile – comfortable, quiet, stable – although what it sounds like to the people on the ground can only be imagined. At these speeds and at this level things happen extremely quickly. But there are two of us in the crew, and a highly intelligent aircraft with a lot of sophisticated equipment to help us. I have started to think of it as a team of three.

We are in the final stages of a bombing mission, and in this air force there is one simple rule, with no exceptions. You are expected to produce 100 per cent success. If you are given a target, you destroy it, so I am looking for a first pass direct hit. It is better than having to make a second pass, when the defences are alert, and better than having to fly the mission all over again.

The mission began nearly two hours ago, with an assigned target, and a careful study of the charts. We are to drop one practice bomb on a target the size of a double bed, on the range out on the sandy flats off East Anglia, at Donna Nook. Before then we shall have flown a route that will take us through the low-level flying area in north-west England. First we need to study the target, to assess the best way to approach it and to leave it. It is no good approaching it directly into a low sun, and we do not want to exit the target area over dangerous or sensitive points such as surface-to-air missile sites, or, in our case, local hospitals and villages. Mark in a good initial point from where we can start our run in to the target, and work back from there.

This is a training sortie, and the mission will take us nearly 600 miles. We need to select the turning points along the route, all the way from take-off to target. Study the danger areas on the map, and check the NOTAMS (Notices to Air Men) to make sure there are no notified obstacles for the day. We shall need turning points, and fix points, where the navigator can check our position and make sure that the navigation system is working correctly or, if not, update it.

Mark in all the selected points on the 1:500,000 scale map, then lay the map under the transparent sheet on the planning table in the operations room. This is navigational planning in the computer age. A small rolling ball device, with a glass window with crossed hairs, together with its related computer, form the basis of the planning machinery. To set up the system, lay the cross in the window over any convenient point on the map, and type in the coordinates on the computer. An intersection in the grid lines is a simple and useful point. Move the rolling ball to another intersection some distance away on the map, and type in the coordinates of that one. The computer tells us that it has registered our entry, and confirms that it knows the scale of the map on which we are working. Now all we have to do is move the rolling ball so that the cross in the window covers each of our predetermined points, and press the appropriate key. A key indicates whether the point is a turning point, or a fix point, or a target. As each key is pressed the computer screen writes up the coordinates for us, and confirms the type of point that we have selected by assigning it a symbol – A to M for turning points, numbers for fix points, and X, Y and Z for targets.

The computer is also programmed to handle elevation. One of the fixed points is the exact position in which the aircraft sits on the flight line. Another is the threshold of the runway from which it will take off. When we enter the details of the target, we also need to enter its height above sea level. Then, as the aircraft climbs and descends, its inertial navigation systems will read those changes, and so long as it knows the height it started from, it will know at any stage its height above the target — essential information when it comes to delivering a bomb.

Our next simple task is to specify the route we want by typing the symbols in the order we want the aircraft to follow them — for example A,B,C, 1, D,E,F, X,Y. Now we can preview the entire route, to make sure that it is a sensible way to fly, by pressing the button marked PLAN. Tap out a few more details, then load the route on to the cassette recorder beside the computer. Take the cassette with us to the aircraft. Load it into the player in the cockpit, and the aircraft is ready to take us along the route we have planned from the apron to the target.

In the Tornado, the plan is usually completed by the navigator, or by the pilot and navigator working together. The two work as a team, sharing the workload and keeping a wary eye out for other aircraft. In war we might encounter enemy marauders; in peace it could be aircraft from other stations, looking to embarrass us with a successful bounce, or private aircraft, who share the airspace and might be terrified to find a Tornado thundering across their track 1,000 ft below them.

We are in the final segment of training, at the Tactical Weapons Conversion Unit at RAF Honington, near Bury St Edmunds. In the course of three months here, we have concentrated on the art of weapons delivery. In more hours of ground school, and hours of flying the Tornado, we have been introduced to the variety of weapons which our aircraft is able to carry and deliver, learned the various modes in which the aircraft can operate, and practised the skills of gunnery and bombing on the range, and of advanced combat manoeuvres against other aircraft. Most of our flying has been in the front cockpit of the aircraft, with an instructor flying in the rear seat. He will also have flown in the front seat, with a student navigator in the rear seat. Soon the two of us — student pilot and student navigator — will be brought together to fly as a new professional team. We are coming close to being masters of the aircraft and its systems.

We are also coming close to the end of the course, and today we have to demonstrate our ability to plan and fly a complete simulated attack profile.

We have the route loaded into the cassette, and the cassette in the navigation computer. Taxi out to the threshold. Obtain take-off clearance. Advance the throttles to full afterburner, brakes off, and the Tornado proceeds with stately power down the runway and rotates smoothly into flight. Gear up when airborne, wings to mid-sweep, throttles to normal, and we are into the most exhilarating flight offered by any of the aircraft we have encountered in our career to date.

To the observer on the ground an afterburner take-off, and the initial climb, provides the sights and sounds of awesome power and infinite threat – the combustion glowing as orange as the sun in the jet pipe, and the air vibrating with the power of the thrust. But inside the cockpit, all that fuss is left behind. The student pilot is in command of a weapons system that makes fewer and fewer customary demands on him. It is a helpful aircraft. It is designed to remove the difficult parts of flying. It leaves the pilot free to concentrate on the tasks that will lead to the completion of the mission. Every time.

In smooth and effortless silence the aircraft powers up to 7,000 ft, well above the levels of the military air traffic zones, and below the airways which throw their complex net over Britain and the Continent.

Typically, a mission will be high/low/high. Travel to the target area at high level to economise on fuel, drop down to low level for a dash to the target, deliver the weapon, recover to high level and return to base. With a typical bomb load the aircraft can attack targets at 850 nautical miles (nm) distance. Today's sortie will take us through about 650 nm.

At 7,000 ft the aircraft continues on its seemingly omnipotent way. Below us two Tornado F–3s, light grey against the brown landscape, take off from RAF Coningsby. Set the speed at 420 knots for the cruise, and trim the aircraft. To stay VMC (in visual meteorological conditions) I thread our way among the cumulus tops. On a peaceful day it is a magical, magisterial experience. We have seven tons of fuel on board and four practice bombs. They are designed to simulate a retarded bomb on delivery – the kind that have a parachute attached to allow you to fly clear of the debris of the explosion. The navigator in the rear has selected the navigation mode, and in the head-up-display two parallel lines show where the planned track is. If I felt like it, I could fly religiously along between those lines, and I would travel to each turning point, unerringly, one after the other. But so long as I have the information available when I need it, I can depart freely from the planned track, picking it up again at any time I want to. The two lines are a great comfort. So is the moving map on the display down in front of me. It can be set to 'north up', in which case the aircraft is at the centre of the circular display, or to 'normal'. Switching between them sends the map spinning, and as it sorts itself out on 'normal' it places my aircraft at the bottom, and aligns the map so that I am flying directly up it, the way pilots orient their own maps all the time. And down by my right knee I still have the map I prepared in the planning room, to refer to should I need it.

A hundred or so miles north and we are planning to drop to 250 ft to cross the Pennines. Roll the aircraft to inverted, pull through into a dive, roll upright, and level out as we approach the height we want. Keep threading a route round the villages. I can keep an eye on the two parallel lines, and on the moving map. Together they give me a perfect picture of where we are, and a perfect guide to where we want to go. I can concentrate on the flight, and on the lookout.

Just for a boost of confidence building, I decide to use the terrain-following radar. That little box of tricks allows the Tornado to fly low at night or in bad weather or low cloud. Select the 'ride' I want – hard, soft, or intermediate – and engage it. Then engage auto-steer. Now I can take my hands off the controls altogether. The aircraft goes into a kind of headstrong wilful mood, following the ground contours, and working out for itself the best way to get back on track. The selection of the ride is not merely for the pilot's comfort. It governs the amount of g – the unit for measuring gravitational pull on the pilot – that the aircraft will accept, and thereby how closely it follows the contours of the ground below. In war a flight that follows the ground contours, however bumpy the ride might be, is better than a smooth ride that evens them out. The aircraft flies along like a porpoise,

11

whooshing up in magnificent arcs over the hills, and plunging down into the valleys. It has the intelligence to read the contours ahead, and to work out when one appears to be coming into its track. If a conflict with the ground is likely, it will give a fly-up command, and resolve the conflict. Instructors have a nasty habit of frightening new students by taking their hands off the controls, waving them in the air, and demonstrating that the aircraft is flying itself.

Now we have flown almost the length of England, and from one coast to the other. To keep the student on his toes, the instructor in the rear cockpit throws in a diversion. 'Let's divert to Warton.' Out with the book; read the frequency, and call their tower. 'Tornado GR1, Hotel Oscar Two Nine. Ten miles north-east of you at 750 ft. Request flyover and one circuit for practice.' He identifies us on his radar and gives us permission to make a pass at 400 ft and a circuit, and information about a private aircraft on finals for the secondary runway. We arrive at an acceptable initial point, line up with Runway Two Five, and storm in at 400 ft, then turn and climb to 1,000 ft, fly downwind, tip in to finals, and drop down to 400 ft for a second pass. Then away out over the sea, beyond the 'chainlink' where the book shows we are not allowed to fly, then bank hard right and north along the Blackpool sea front and across the expanse of Morecombe Bay to rejoin our original route.

The parallel lines on the head-up display are telling us that we are to the left of the planned track, but flying to intercept it. We are rapidly approaching the mountains of the Lake District. At 420 knots there is no time for hesitation, so choose a valley, and position the aircraft to enter the low-flying area. Today the air is so sparklingly clear you could navigate with one eye and no map, let alone without technological aids.

On such a day a training sortie is more of a pleasure than a trial. In the Operational Conversion Unit, pilots and students are allowed to enjoy this kind of flying. It gives them the chance to learn about the aircraft's performance characteristics and its systems, in a relatively unpressed atmosphere. And such days are rare enough to make it worthwhile enjoying them. Ahead the mountains are totally clear of cloud, bathed in spring sunshine beneath a deep blue sky. The peaks, way above our level, are draped in snow, and in an instant we are through the gap in the hills and flying north along the familiar lines of Windermere. From 250 ft the houses on either side of the lake look close enough to drop in for a visit. A passenger boat leaves its wake below us, and we bank on to a knife-edge as a kind of greeting. Cars and visitors surround the local beauty spots, pink faces turned up to watch us flash overhead. Langdale and its pikes, familiar from a dozen climbing visits, are off to the left. We turn up the dogleg half-way along Windermere, bank to look at another boat, then shoot off the end, over the passes, and down again to 250 ft above Thirlmere. The mountains tower above, flecked black and white with rock and snow. For the climber on foot, an ascent to the tops and a visit to a couple of summits is a six-hour outing. The Tornado reduces time by a process of merciless compaction. Keswick comes up ahead and we bank hard and pull g to avoid overflying the houses. Then Derwentwater, and suddenly, after only five minutes of flying, we shoot out from the knot of mountains and lakes into a landscape that is flat with fields and farms below us.

That is when the student pilot begins to understand that he has sampled one of the great rewards of the fast jet pilot's trade – flying a high-speed aircraft over some of the world's most spectacular landscapes. And he has fallen victim to one of its great paradoxes – that it all happens at such a speed and in such an intensity of pressured activity there is scarcely time to enjoy it.

Back to the business in hand. The navigation display indicates a turn to the right on to the next leg, and we fly along the edge of the Solway Firth. That is Scotland just over the other side, and Phantom country. Sure enough, a smudge just above the horizon in the distance, 10–12 miles away, turns out to be a fighter from one of the Scottish bases. He shows no interest in us, and gets smaller. At least we are becoming alert to spotting potential enemies at reasonable distances. Then, as if to put us in our places, we are startled by a shadow tracking across the fields in front of us. A light aeroplane is poised overhead and we flash beneath him. We should have seen him earlier. One black mark.

We have travelled, in the phonetic language of the airman, through turning points Alpha, Bravo, Charlie, and Delta. There is a short leg from turning point Foxtrot to Golf on 153 degrees, then back on to the brown landscape over the moors, cutting across England parallel to the motorway. Then south. Here a vast ridge gives us a feature to follow. It is essential to good flying that the student pilot learns to avoid slavishly following the parallel tracks in the head-up display. The better technique is to use our initiative and fly with discretion to take advantage of the ground features, using the navigation displays as an aid, not as a master. Another turn, and in the distance the twin towers of the great Humber bridge come into view. We cross the river to the right of them, far below the level of the bridge tops. We have picked up a low-level route, and we begin to approach the coast and the bombing range at Donna Nook. The targets are clear bright red on the grey shore away to the left. Fly south, report to the range officer, follow an earlier aircraft round, wings over and pull g to turn north, roll the wings level as we come parallel with the coast.

'Select weapons pack one.'

I have called for the weapons system to be set up for a level bombing run, using a retarded bomb.

'Select Attack.' Behind me the weapons systems operator – for that is a better title than navigator – punches the switches on his computer to give me the attack mode.

'Select target.'

On the head-up display in front of me, the faint green lines appear. There is a narrow V. The target is a bright red raft, looking about the size of a double bed.

'Stabilise the radar, please.' In the rear seat the navigator checks his radar against the moving map in front of him. The coastline is a useful fix. If the navigation system has drifted at all, the radar picture will show it up as a discrepancy between the line of the coast on the moving map, and the radar return from the same area. All he has to do is slew the picture across the map until the two coincide.

The aircraft is now set up. If I wanted to now I could switch on the terrain-following radar, flick aside the safety cage on the bomb-release trigger, and pull the trigger. The aircraft would know the position and height of the target, would read its own height, and would know the characteristics of the weapon I had selected, and would release it for me at the right time. I decided that that was rather too easy, so I have opted for a visual attack.

The run is south to north. I need to report to the range control officer. 'Hotel Oscar November Two Nine, for level attack as scheduled.'

'Hotel Oscar November Two Nine, one ahead of you. Which way do you want to clear?'

'We'll clear to the south and east. Two Nine.'

'Two Nine. Aircraft ahead has cleared. Proceed with your attack.'

'Two Nine.'

I advance the throttle and let the speed stabilise at 480 knots. The height is moving slightly around 240, 250, 260 knots. It doesn't matter. It is much more important to keep an eye on the target ahead. It is slightly off to the right. 'I have the radar.' I take control of the radar for the attack phase from the navigator in the rear cockpit. His job is done for the moment. The target shows as a blip on the screen. I have it in my control, so I can slew the cross on the radar on to the target, and press the stabiliser button. Now I have updated the aircraft's knowledge of the target's position. I could have selected a new target at will, say an armoured column during a reconnaissance mission.

Select the fix/attack button on the navigation display. Toggle the switch to give us target number one. In the head-up display the bomb-fall line appears. Now comes the really clever part. The target is also clearly marked. Adjust the radar to position the cross over the target, and press the button to stabilise it in the centre of the display. Now the target information is updated. With target selected, its position is marked by the two short horizontal dashes in the head-up display. And the bomb-fall line hangs down from between them. We are approaching the target fast. But with the bomb-fall line, and the target in the gap between the two short lines, all we have to do is fly the aircraft towards that gap, and we will lay the bomb-fall line over the target. Watch the small cross move up the bomb line. Somewhere in the bowels of the aircraft the main computer has stored all the information for the weapon we have selected, including its trajectory, the air pressure, our airspeed, and our altitude, and is working away at thirty calculations per second to determine the Continuously Computed Impact Point (CCIP). That is precisely the point where the bomb will hit the ground. Time to uncage the bomb-release trigger, and press it to commit the bomb for release. Now everything is lined up. All I have to do is keep flying the aircraft so that the bomb-fall line runs through the target point. No drama. No noise. Just an accurate pass over the target, and the range officer reports, 'Delta Hotel, Two Nine.'

I slam the wings over and pull 4 g and climb to escape out to the south-east over the grey North Sea.

Delta Hotel. Delta Hotel. It is the phonetic alphabet for DH: Direct Hit. The phrase has a magical ring to a fighter pilot – rewarding, and satisfying. Delta Hotel. I like the sound of it. I have scored a direct hit, on my first flight in command of a Tornado. It is time to go back to base, so advance the power to engage the afterburner, and with a feeling of overjoyed liberation, pull back the stick to climb the aircraft. In not much more than ten seconds it has reached 10,000 ft. So invert it, pull through to level off, and roll it wings level again. And ease back the power to begin a gentle and fuel-saving cruise home.

At this stage in the course, after nearly four years of learning to fly and to operate the weapons system to which the student pilot has been assigned, there is none of the sense of pass or fail. Just a thorough debrief between professionals. If, regrettably, he cannot handle the complexities of the system, and it looks as if he will not be able to handle the additional intensity of doing all this flying in a war, one of the instructors will take him on one side and discuss his shortcomings with him, and if necessary take the problem up through the ranks to his station commander. He could eventually be re-assigned to another flying role, with lower demands and fewer pressures. But that is in nobody's interests. Apart from the monumental investment in him as a fighter pilot, for which the Royal Air Force would justifiably like to see some return, any inadequacies should have been exposed at an earlier stage, and any necessary adjustments in his career made then.

On the other hand, if the student pilot has progressed satisfactorily through the weapons conversion unit, he is now ready to join a squadron.

# 2

## Two Days in a Hangar

Acquiring the qualifications which entitle you to take charge of a multi-million dollar machine, equipped with weapons which could destroy people in thousands, and which, improperly handled, could precipitate an international crisis, is not easy. Nor is the qualification available on request. Nor, for that matter, can you achieve it simply with hard work. It requires much more than that. It is not easy to define what it does take, but if you add up the sum total of all that the experts say, you will probably conclude that to become a fighter pilot, you need a unique combination of fitness, aptitude, determination, co-ordination, intelligence, sound common sense, extrovert good nature, courage, tenacity . . . the list goes on.

And you need to demonstrate these qualities at every stage in the qualifying process or, to be strictly accurate, before you even begin.

First, you have to pass the rigorous selection tests. To do that you merely have to endure two days of unbearable high-pressure torment, while keeping your mental and physical faculties intact. You have to stay alert and enthusiastic while solving an unending series of apparently insoluble problems. And you have to keep your self-control and good humour while your chance of success seem to be falling apart in your hands. In other words, you simply have to shine.

The Officer & Aircrew Selection Centre is an acknowledged world authority on the process of manpower selection, not only for flying and for the armed forces, but for management in general. It used to be at RAF Biggin Hill, the best known of the Battle of Britain airfields, but has recently moved to the centre of Royal Air Force officer training at RAF Cranwell. Every year, over 8,000

17

young men and women report to the selection centre, many of them desperately committed to a flying career since their first infant acquaintance with the magical world of aeroplanes. Half of them will be sent home before they have got half-way through the course, and in many cases before they are half-way through the first morning. They either lack aptitude, or are medically unsuitable, either with deficient eyesight, or with the wrong size of frame, whether too small or too large.

Of the half who survive the initial stages, about a quarter will be offered places in officer training at the end of the two-day selection process. The Royal Air Force recruits about a thousand officers a year, in various branches. Most of them start off wanting to be pilots, but few find their way into the branch that was their first choice. Many reveal qualities more suited to other branches. Of the thousand or so each year who do succeed, many will have been rejected at their first try: some will be on their third, fourth, or even fifth visits to the selection centre.

The Royal Air Force has to be tough in its selection process. The officers who carry out the selection are benevolent. Anybody, they acknowledge, who submits himself at an age between sixteen and twenty-three to this tough brand of testing and selection, must have some qualities that the service could use. On the other hand, barring accidents, they are offering secure employment for anything up to sixteen years, and possibly for life. They have to be certain that the candidates are good. And they have to be right. That obligation puts a duty on them to be ruthless in seeking out, identifying, and exposing a candidate's weaknesses, which is why officer selection can be a harrowing process. It can also, if the candidate is doing well, be enjoyable. Either way, it is fair, searching, and accurate.

The tests divide into two parts: the first, largely objective in nature; the second, more subjective, as the selection board officers make their own assessments of the abilities and potential of the individual.

Report first to the computer room. It looks like the familiar language laboratory, with soft lighting and banks of cubicles screened from each other. Each cubicle houses a computer. Sit down before your screen, make yourself comfortable, and press any key to start. The computer asks you to confirm your name and age, and almost promises to be your friend for the next four-and-a-half hours. It will certainly know a lot about you at the end of that time.

The first test makes you feel almost like a pilot. A small control stick sits in front of you, just as in an aircraft. Any young person who has played computer games will know what to do, but the computer delivers its instructions anyway. The stick controls a white dot, and your job is to move that white dot from side to side, so that it intercepts a string of red dots as they stream steadily down the screen.

First, you have a few minutes for practice. It seems straight-forward enough. Now press the 'move' key to start the first of three exercises, and the red dots appear. Move the stick to intercept them. Yes, this is like being a pilot. When you hit one, a gentle beep gives you encouragement. The string of dots snakes steadily down the screen, veering gently, and occasionally dividing as if round an island in a stream, giving more targets along one route than on the other. If you look ahead and anticipate the bends in the line, you can give yourself more chances. Unfortunately, the control stick seems to have a mind of its own, as its rate of change alters with the movements you make. Small shifts produce small movements of the dot, and large ones progressively larger move-ments, so that it takes some rapid accommodation to predict the amount of movement required, to anticipate the changes of direction in the stream of targets, and to move your stick accordingly.

You get on to the line of dots. A few beeps sound. Elation. The dots move to the right. The machine goes silent. You move the stick further to try to intercept them, but not by enough. So you move your stick more, and your white dot goes shooting off to the side. By the time you get it back, the red dots have moved, then moved again. Your hands begin to sweat, and tremble. Your whole career depends on this damned spot. If you cannot fly this silly white dot on this simple computer, you convince yourself, you can hardly expect to be invited to fly a jet fighter. But stop thinking like that, and concentrate.

The first test ends, with ominously more silences than beeps. Depressed, you punch the 'move' button to start the second sequence. Things seem easier, and you hear a lot of beeps, then you lose your touch, and silence ensues, a long, disapproving silence, while you manoeuvre the spot across the screen and the wayward red dots wander elusively and contemptuously down their course. You can feel failure in the air, and you begin to tremble nervously. Then you acknowledge defeat. Throw it away. Who cares if we can't intercept dots? We'll go and be policemen instead. Accepting your fate makes the trembling stop, and you relax. That brings back a measure of control, and you start to intercept the dots and hear the beeps again. Perhaps there's a chance. You try harder, and that makes you tighten up, and you start to miss the dots again. You are half-way through the third and last stream, when you begin to feel fatigue. Now you twig the secret. Concentrate. Concentrate and relax. They are conflicting demands, but you can handle them. Relax. Concentrate. While you have been working this out you have passed through the stream of dots from right to left and from left to right half a dozen times, and heard all too few beeps. Then the screen goes blank, and the message comes up: 'Test complete'.

On such events are promising careers made and broken. You could have been a guardian of the peace, perhaps a war hero, ultimately Chief of the Air Staff, certainly the pilot of a Tornado at Mach 2, living in the officers' mess at RAF Coningsby. That was how you saw yourself, until your lamentable performance with this damnable little moving dot let you down. And that was in the first ten minutes of two days of tests.

Before you have time to contemplate how you will commit suicide, the computer invites you to take your second test. If hand and eye co-ordination was difficult, try hand, eye and foot co-ordination. A cross appears in the middle of the screen, together with the familiar spot. This time, your control column moves the spot only up and down the screen. Move the control column forwards, and the dot goes down. Move it back towards you, and the dot goes up. Try it, the computer suggests. You try it. It seems easy enough. Under your table are two pedals, just like the rudder pedals of an aeroplane. Slot your feet comfortably on to them, your heels on the lips provided. The pedals move the spot laterally. Press with the left foot to move it to the left, and the right foot to move it to the right. All you have to do is keep the spot in the centre of the cross.

Ready? There is no point in delaying your moment of commitment; you might as well get the agony over. So press the 'move' button to start the exercise. The spot starts to the left of centre, and you move it gently to the right. No, not with the control stick, idiot. Use your feet. Too far. Move it back again, and that is a touch too far this way. Then it goes up the screen. You ease the stick back to get it down again, and it shoots up. No! Forwards to move it down. Damn! It moves down. Then it moves down and off to the right. You had forgotten about your rudder pedals again. You kick with the left foot to get it back. It centralises. But now you have forgotten about the control stick. The dot has drifted down, and away to the side again. Hand and foot co-ordination. That's the point of this exercise. Use them both. Remember that. The spot suddenly centralises. Is that me or is it the machine being kind to me? It stays in the centre, right on the cross, with only gentle pressures, then veers off to the left and high. You pull back and press with the left foot. Wrong! Push forwards and press with the right foot. You get it back to the centre. It seems to want to stay there. This test seems easier than the last. Then off goes the dot again, wild and elusive. You ease it back into the centre with a little self-discipline, and muscle control, and relaxed handling, and concentration. Do you think we could ask to go back and try the first test again? We are getting rather good at this. Damn! There it goes again. Bring it rapidly back . . . and hold it there, with hand and foot. Then the screen goes blank. It is the end of the pilot control-column tests.

Go on to the instrument appreciation test. Press the 'move' button when you are ready. OK? The computer draws for you, one at a time, the basic instruments which a pilot will see on the panel in front of him. (In fact, they are not in quite the familiar order, just to reduce the advantage of experience.) First, the altimeter, with an explanation of what it shows, with a couple of examples to call up at your own pace, so that you really understand. Then an attitude indicator, with your own little index aeroplane and the line of the horizon, and a few examples to show when it is climbing, and descending, and when it is turning, both while it is level and while it is climbing or descending, and whether it is turning to the right or left.

Next, the airspeed indicator, which reads like any standard instrument, provided you know which way round it is going, and can estimate the divisions. Then there is the vertical speed indicator, which shows whether you are level, climbing or descending, and how rapidly you are doing so. There is also your direction indicator, which looks much like a compass with the cardinal points marked. And finally the turn-and-bank indicator. Now this is complicated. It has two needles, pointing downwards and upwards, to show, as it were, six and twelve o'clock. The bottom needle shows your direction of turn and the rate at which you are turning. The top needle shows your balance in the turn. Pilots (some pilots at least) will know just what this means. Newcomers may have difficulty. In a correct turn, the bottom needle will be angled in the direction of your turn, with the upwards-pointing needle centralised because your turn is balanced. If you are slipping into a left turn the top needle will be canted left. If you are skidding outwards from the left turn, the top needle will be canted out at an angle to the right. You could be flying straight, without any turn, but with the top needle showing an angle of bank, because you have one wing low. Got that?

Right. Multiple choice. All you have to do is read the instruments, and choose one from a set of sentences which describes what the aeroplane is doing. For example: the aeroplane is climbing rapidly in a left turn at 260 knots and slipping into the turn. You read the instruments as fast as you can to check the accuracy of the statement, and punch its number.

By the time you have completed a few of these you will know – and the Royal Air Force will know – whether or not you can understand instruments.

It is not all. There is a second part to this test. For this you need only two instruments – the attitude indicator, with its horizon and its little aeroplane symbol to show whether you are climbing or descending and at what angle of bank, and a very simple direction indicator, marked with N,E,S and W. Below this pair of instruments are six computer-drawings of aircraft, each with a number. The aircraft are travelling south if they are shown coming towards you, north if away from you, and east if shown moving to the right. Perfectly logical. The symbol will show if the aircraft is climbing, and banked to the left, or descending with wings level, or any other combination. You have sixty questions in twenty-five minutes. Press 'move' to begin; press the relevant number key when you have decided which drawing represents the aircraft indicated in the two instruments, and press 'move' to bring up the next question. Work rapidly through the questions.

The sequence begins with a simple one. Then another simple

one. Then they become more complicated, as the aircraft seems to be climbing and turning away from you towards the right of the screen, and the instruments show an aircraft in a climb, banked to the left, and travelling in a direction north of north-east. You punch number 5 and 'move', and press on.

By the time the 'time to go' clock has changed from minutes to seconds, and the screen at last shows 'test complete', you have seen aircraft in more conditions of flight than you ever knew existed, and you have no idea whether your interpretation of the instruments and their correlation with the symbols was based on your clear vision or on utter confusion.

Not to worry. By now you have forgotten your nervousness and thrown away all thoughts that you might have a flying career ahead of you, and you are content to pass the time doing tests. You have completed the three that relate directly to pilot aptitude. There are twenty-one others. Some will reveal your aptitude for navigation. Some are computerised versions of general intelligence tests. Some test your mathematical capability, some your spatial orientation, which is extremely important to a fighter pilot; some your left/right co-ordination. All aspects of your make-up which might affect your ability to perform as an officer and an aviator will be scrutinised in detail by the computer. Not least, it will test your ability to keep going and respond to challenges thrown at you when you really feel like putting a fist through its screen and going home.

The tests add up to one of the most modern and sophisticated aptitude assessment techniques in the world. They have been validated against the performance of pilots in service, so at least you know that if you cannot satisfy the requirements of those tests, you will not be able to function as a pilot at the level the Royal Air Force requires. As you escape from the computer room back to the candidates' lounge for a cup of coffee, the central computer has already decided your fate, and a print-out of your performance is ready, with scores on your individual tests, their weighted values according to the importance of the test, and their individual relationship to the scores of the rest of the population.

How did we manage? On the pilot aptitude test, we achieved a score right on the average for the population as a whole, just good enough to squeeze through into acceptance for pilot training, given adequate scores in the other tests. But those raw aptitude scores have yet to be adjusted, to give a 'P', or pilot, score. That process will be performed, again by the computer, according to an arcane process known as regression equations, to take account of your age, your performance in the interview still to come, and any experience you might have in powered aeroplanes, which could be a considerable help.

Your next test is the medical, to establish two things. Are you fit, and will you fit? Testing your physical condition is a three-hour process, at the end of which the doctors will know whether your eyesight, hearing, heart, and everything else about you are up to standard for the Royal Air Force. If you seek a flying career, you will also have to fit into the cockpit, and all your relevant limbs are measured for length. A pilot too short in the spine to see over the cockpit coaming, too tall to get his helmet under the canopy, or too long in the thigh to allow his knees to clear the instrument panel in the event of an ejection, cannot go flying for a living in this service. Ninety-five per cent of the population fall within the acceptable range.

Following your medical, you go on to your interview. Two members of the selection board painstakingly study your file before you are called, looking at your application form, your school reports, and any details of previous visits to the selection centre. By the time the duty sergeant shows you into the interview room, they know enough about you to begin a discussion. The questions start simply enough, about you, your upbringing, your school, your activities in school, your activities out of school, your travel, your interests. What sports do you play? What clubs do you belong to? Then the subjects become less simple. What do you know about the aircraft in the NATO inventory? What do you know about the latest fighter aircraft from the Warsaw Pact? What is the role of the Royal Air Force? How do you think the changes in Eastern Europe will affect the role of the Royal Air Force? Your knowledge is subtly probed, as are your views, your depth of thinking, and the sources of your information, such as the newspapers you read.

Two officers have talked to you for more than half an hour, and at the end of that time each has formed his assessment of your performance. Is your knowledge of current affairs genuine, and your grasp of the subjects you have talked about sound? Have you a lively interest in aircraft and the Royal Air Force, and have you done any reading about the subject? Have you done anything to develop your interest in this career before presenting yourself for selection? Are you bright, articulate, genuine, strongly motivated, and well rounded? Have you shown plenty of initiative at your school, university or polytechnic, and have you demonstrated your independence, and your spirit of adventure? Or are you, as one selection board officer lamented, a 'plank'? The service has no place for 'planks'.

The only things that are of no consequence are your political views, and your accent. The Royal Air Force looks for bright, fit, articulate young people, who are interested in flying. It also wants those who are interested in much more than flying. The narrow-minded flying freak will not get far as a Royal Air Force officer, because the life of an officer calls for qualities beyond a passion for flying.

By now you are half-way through the process, and your selection board knows the results of your aptitude tests, details of your medical examination, and the marks you have been awarded for your performance in the interview. Those items add up to a Part 1 assessment, and if you clearly did not measure up to the requirement, you will be called for interview, debriefed, and sent home. Half of the original intake go home at this stage. Your aim is to be in the other half. If you make it, you will get a substantial lunch, and a complete change of emphasis.

From now on you are performing not only on your own, but with others, and much of the coming assessment, Part 2, is designed to find out how well you integrate with a team, and how well you are likely to be able to lead one.

The coming tests are decidedly physical, so you are given a change of clothes. The air force issues an anonymous olive-drab overall with a white vest to go over it. The vest carries what will from now on be your own identity. It has a letter, to identify your syndicate of six, and a number, to identify you individually. I am no longer David Mason, but G3. Leave personal belongings on the table in front of you ... watch, wallet, pens, earrings (earrings!). Fasten your cuffs down with the Velcro strip at the wrists, and tuck your trousers into your socks. Secure the vest under the epaulettes so that if you are turned upside down – correction, *when* you are turned upside down – you will not be rendered sightless.

Now to the hangar. This houses the Royal Air Force's version of a cross between an assault course, a modernist sculpture exhibition, and an adventure playground. A dozen or so groups of sundry apparatus are fixed to the concrete floor – wooden boxes, oil drums, bars, old tyres hanging on ropes – all quite simple, but ominously surrounded by soft rubber mats. Each exercise is different, to give plenty of scope, and to avoid second- and third-time candidates coming equipped with all the answers. The aims, and the rules, are simple. All six people in the syndicate have to make their way from the start line to the finish without touching the floor. Any part of the equipment painted black is out of bounds; everything painted white is in bounds. A few basic items are offered to help you along – a couple of planks, a length of cord, a crate. The two main problems are that the planks are never long enough to reach from one in-bounds item to another, and that all the equipment has to be taken over the course along with the six members of the group. You can leave nothing behind. The tasks all look impossible – every one. Yet miraculously syndicate after syndicate completes them within the time allowed, usually twenty minutes.

The first exercise in Part 2 is known, with unconscious humour, as 'leaderless'. The six candidates in the syndicate are briefed together, and launched on to the first course. The ones with the good ideas soon emerge. So do the ones who are assertive. So do the ones who are assertive but have only bad ideas. Completing the exercise calls for a broad understanding of the principles of levers, strong spatial awareness, and physical courage. Even the first gap, from the start line at floor level to a high box, looks unbridgeable, but by adapting a plank with a lot of support at one end, the group produces a cantilever and starts precariously to inch members across it. Somebody remembers to move the equipment forwards, and the oil drum and crate are manoeuvred over. That leaves a man stranded, still behind the start line. The braver souls invent a solution, standing on one end of the plank which pokes out over the gap towards him. It looks unbridgeable, but he reaches forward, leaps on to it, and scrambles across. It holds. Ahead two members have decided to tie two planks together. With one piece of string the result looks shaky. Two would be an engineer's minimum, but if they position the planks the right way round, it will hold as a makeshift bridge. With balance, and nerve, and imagination, they end up at the other side. One or two have made exceptional contributions. One or two have begun to emerge as leaders. One or two have been distinguished by their anonymity. The facts are noted. The 'leaderless' exercise has shown how the candidates can work within a group. Can they make their personalities felt? Do they listen to others and make good use of somebody else's ideas? Are they overbearing? Humourless?

Next it is back to the syndicate room for a class exercise. The aims are similar – to search out confidence, intelligence, nerve. But this is not physical at all. It is a group discussion. Form your chairs into a semicircle. Imagine you are in a pub or club or round the fireside. The topic for discussion is this: it is not the role of the Church to interfere in politics. I repeat: it is not the role of the Church to interfere in politics. Begin your discussion . . . now. Some candidates dive straight in. Others hang back, shy and reticent. There is no need to hurry, because there is plenty of time to listen to others and still make your points. But make your points you must. The ones who continue to hang back get nowhere. The ones who talk incessantly also risk a low assessment. Some are talked straight over by the rest of the syndicate. Others have no trouble in making themselves heard.

The selection board officers are making notes and forming assessments throughout. Can Number One think on his feet? Has Number Four something to say and is it sensible? Number Six is quite assertive but is also prepared to listen and picks up other speakers' points. Number Two seemed completely mesmerised by it all. And Number Three seemed to have interesting views and expressed them clearly, but he tended to fade towards the end. Small wonder! After over half an hour of supervised but undirected free discussion on three separate and entirely unprepared topics, a candidate might be entitled to fade, especially if he made the mistake of imagining that he was being selected for flying as a fighter-pilot. At this stage he is being selected primarily for training as an officer. It is worth remembering that.

It is worth remembering it also during the last test of the afternoon, which is a syndicate exercise to work out a solution to a complicated theoretical problem. The Royal Air Force seems to have a highly developed talent for creating hypothetical situations which are both interesting and challenging. The syndicate members are given a drawing, which helps to set the scene, and a description, with a calculation aid if appropriate. You are in charge of an oil station overseas, with fifty European workers, twenty locally recruited workers, thirty women, and fifteen children on the station. The local population is in revolt, and an attack on your station is imminent. The local workers are unreliable. You have a twelve-seat aeroplane and a four-seat aeroplane, plus four trucks and a fire-engine, but no more fuel. You are given their ranges, passenger-carrying capacities, and speeds. Fuel, arms, and ammunition are available at the next station, ninety miles away. A British destroyer with fifty Royal Marines on board left port fifty miles away last night, but you do not know in what direction. Sabotage has destroyed the local power supply so your station radio is out. What is your plan?

A ten-minute discussion among the syndicate should produce some good ideas, and will certainly knock down the more ludicrous ones. Those ideas that seemed like good ones but turned out to be impracticable will be revealed by questioning from a selection board officer. How much fuel have you got, Number Three? How far will it take you, Number Four? Number Six, how many women and children will the aeroplane carry if it is designed for twelve adults? How long will that trip take, Number One? Everybody is challenged, on their understanding of the question, on their ability to plan, on their calculations, on their capacity to re-calculate under pressure – above all, on their performance under pressure. Blank looks are not accepted. Brave attempts at rapid and intelligent responses are.

At the end of this long day the candidates are free. Sensible ones relax sensibly: tomorrow the tests which they have so far done with help from the rest of the syndicate will have to be tackled alone. The candidates will need all their courage and concentration, and a very clear head for the next morning.

The individual planning exercise, a replica of the syndicate problem but worked through alone, is among the most difficult of all the tests, and can put candidates under extreme stress. Tears have been shed in the course of this exercise. The candidate has twenty minutes to read the situation, study the map, and come up with his solution. I have been left in charge of a minicab company which owns three vehicles. We have been given three jobs to carry out, and we have three personnel. Average speeds for the vehicles are given, and complexities such as roadworks and delays on jobs are built in. The jobs all have inconvenient load weights and times. How am I going to achieve them all? The solution lies in spotting the probable best use of my vehicles, then carrying out some rapid calculations to back up my intuitive conclusions. The biggest danger is trying to work out every possible combination, to establish a list of preferences. That would get you nowhere in the twenty minutes available. The second biggest danger is opting for a simple and naïve conclusion, which fails to make sensible use of your resources.

Having got as near to a conclusion as time and your brain will allow, you are recalled to the interview room, alone, to face again the searching investigation of the selection board. Surprisingly, they also frequently find themselves under some stress, as they try to keep ahead of the bright candidate, or struggle to understand the workings of the mind of the eccentric. The questions come like a stream of tracer: about your understanding of the problem (it is strange how many fail to read it accurately), about your general plan, about your calculations, with new calculations to make on the spot to test your ability to think and react under stress, about your alternative solutions. And afterwards the assessment. Were you incisive, or did you waffle in response to questions? Could you calculate and recalculate under pressure? Was your thinking flexible and did you listen to suggestions? Did you show a grasp of the problem, and sound judgement, or were you totally illogical? It is not surprising that candidates start the exercise in trepidation, shuffle their feet as their errors are exposed, and end up crying with frustration as the brain overloads. What is surprising is that some candidates sail through the exercise and leave the room with 100 per cent on their assessment sheets.

Now, back to the hangar for your last exercise, to test your ability to command. It is much like the leaderless exercise of the preceding day, except that you will have the chance to take charge. You will face six seemingly impossible vertigo-inducing tests. In five of them you will be part of the team. In the sixth you will perform as leader under the glare of the selectors. When you are leader, you are the only member of the team to be briefed on the exercise, while your team is banished behind screens. You are allowed two minutes, alone, to survey the equipment and the problem. Then you can brief the rest of the group on your plan, and get the exercise under way. Your capacity for leadership is exposed ruthlessly. You will succeed if you can organise your team, encourage them, control them, listen to their suggestions, and demonstrate that you have an instinctive feel for the ideal balance between standing back and giving orders, and involving yourself too closely in the task.

Some groups of six come alive with enthusiasm and enjoyment throughout all six tests. Others flail about with little sense of direction, and no real leadership from any of the candidates.

By now you are virtually exhausted, and your 'board' is coming to an end. There remains only a group pep talk in which the facts of service life are explained briefly to you. 'Should you be selected for training as an officer in the Royal Air Force, you will be expected to wear a jacket and tie in the officers' mess. If the service goes to war, the death penalty applies and if you run from the enemy you will be court-martialled and can be shot.' Now that you know what you are letting yourself in for, you receive a brief individual talk. Here at last you abandon your syndicate letter and number, and assume your name and individuality again. Such relief. Do you want to change your list of career choices, Mr Mason, or the type of commission you are seeking? If you are offered a place, when would you be available? Have you found your treatment here fair and straightforward? Then, thank you, and good luck.

Your selectors still have work to do. They have to agree, two of them, on your marks for performance in the command exercise which you have just completed. They also have to report on your personal qualities, as they have found them in all the Part 2 tests which they have supervised. Have you been uninvolved, unenthusiastic, easily over-ruled, out of your depth? Is your approach to teamwork abrasive, uncooperative, intolerant? Physically, are you unfit or overweight, lacking in courage, hesitant? Are you unassertive or indecisive in your leadership skills, and underconfident and ineffective? In terms of intelligence are you easily confused, with poor mental agility and weak judgement, and do you become slow and inaccurate under pressure? How should your Part 2 selectors mark you for overall capability? The air force system has a grading structure which balances your strengths against your weaknesses, and ranges from the highest grade, in which you give such an overwhelming display of strengths that you are unlikely to have any trouble with your officer or flying training, to the lowest, where your weaknesses predominate to the extent that you are certainly not going to make the grade as an officer.

Finally, your selectors have to place their opinions before the president of your board, who will make his recommendations to the station commander. He will weigh your performance in your syndicate exercises against your aptitude test results, your medical, and your performance in interview. He will discuss your abilities in detail with the various assessing officers. It is important that he makes the correct decision. If his recommendation is positive, he will shortly send you on to the first part of your training as an officer in the Royal Air Force, perhaps as a fast-jet pilot.

All you have to do is go home, and wait for three weeks while the system deals with your application, and the letter arrives which will determine your future as an aviator.

# 3

## First an Officer, then a Pilot

When, long ago, you first dreamed of piloting your Harrier or Tornado into action against a skilled and determined enemy, you never imagined that you would first have to train to be an infantry platoon commander, a long-distance moorland guide, a general in a bunker, an office manager, a lay magistrate, and a gibbon. But aeroplanes are still a long way off in the career of the intending fighter pilot. First, there is Cranwell.

Royal Air Force College Cranwell, in Lincolnshire, is where all student officers undergo an eighteen-week course before beginning their specialised training for the professional branch which they will join. The course at Cranwell used to be two years. Then long college-type training courses were dropped in the UK services in favour of shorter training periods, and the Royal Air Force entrant can look forward to taking his commission after an intensive, varied, but mercifully short induction known as Initial Officer Training.

A gibbon? Quite a considerable amount of officer training seems to be spent off the ground (without an aeroplane) swinging around in the trees. You will recall spending time trying valiantly to maintain a state of levitation with the aid of planks, ropes, and old car tyres in the selection process. There is more of it in initial officer training, except that here the challenges are out of doors, usually in trees, and the favoured piece of equipment is the pine log. In the woods dotted around the college, small groups of cadets can be seen solving problems that call for them to inch their way across chasms, using logs, planks, lengths of rope, and sundry other items of jetsam.

The main reason for failure among the student officers at Cranwell is lack of self-confidence, which would inevitably reduce their ability to lead as an officer. Your ability to lead is seriously tested when you are given a load of pine logs, a couple of boards, and a length of rope, and asked to get a large heavy load, and yourself, and the nine other students in your flight, from one tree to another, while remaining ten feet off the ground – in total silence. Exercises like that test the skills that the Royal Air Force wants in all its officers, not in its pilots alone.

In Royal Air Force training parlance, it is called effective intelligence. Training for it would transfer neatly into the management training schemes of many industrial companies. It reveals your ability to plan, and your capacity to motivate other people to carry out your plan. Your flight commander will probably throw in a couple of wild cards from time to time, in the form of new conditions for the exercise, to make you re-think your entire approach, in order to see how comfortably you can adapt to changing situations. Leading your flight through a few of these exercises helps you to build what the service describes as a 'confidence platform'.

You will also spend a great deal of time in the gymnasium, getting fit under the stern eye of your PE instructors. Cranwell introduced sports afternoons not long ago, but gave them up because there was no time in the course, and because students were getting all the exercise they could cope with in the formal fitness course in the gymnasium.

And there is drill. Lots of drill. Look around. You are at Cranwell. Do you see students walking around with their hands in their pockets? No. You see students marching, even when they are on their own, their arms swinging to shoulder height. And if they are with other students they march in line.

The fitness, the self-discipline, and the self-confidence built up in the early weeks all help in coping with one of the highlights of the first part of the course. In weeks seven and eight of the eighteen, you spend eight days in your first camp. The Royal Air Force has access to some of the wildest training grounds in the country, which can be very uncomfortable for students living under canvas, winter and summer alike. One area, Otterburn, is so hostile in winter that students are not allowed to use it. The first camp is designed to refine the candidate's leadership qualities and self-confidence, and involves about three exercises per day, in a day which starts at 07.00 and lasts until 22.00. The exercises are usually simple in their aims, but extremely difficult to execute, and each student can expect to take on the role of leader on at least two exercises in the course of the camp.

Camp Two, which arrives in week eleven, is even more entertaining. Between the two camps you will have learned how to handle the 7.6mm self-loading rifle, the main personal weapon in the Royal Air Force. The SLR is gradually being phased out in the British Army, but the Royal Air Force still relies on it. You will have learned how to fire it, and strip it, and clean it, as well as how to handle and use it while wearing a gas mask. It may be a long way from pilot training, but officers destined for all branches of the service undergo training at Cranwell, and any one of them could find himself, or herself, leading the defence of a remote station against enemy attack.

Gradually, as the course progresses, individuals begin to shine, and are given opportunities to show their gifts, usually by way of extra responsibilities. 'Cadet executives' are appointed from among the cadets, and they have to give many of the briefings that were formerly given by the course instructors.

Here is your task. The war is on. As flight commander, you are to set up a vehicle checkpoint to stop and examine vehicles, check the identity of the occupants, and search any vehicle and its contents if you have grounds for suspicion. If any enemy are encountered, you are to capture prisoners for interrogation by HQ staff. If you are lucky, you will have been given your task on the previous day and have had time to prepare it in detail overnight. But the camp does not always run to schedule, and on some tasks you will be lucky if you have more than a few minutes. Given enough effective intelligence, and bags of self-confidence, you will be able to evolve a plan which takes account of all eventualities, and you should be able to put it across persuasively and convincingly to a group of relatively indifferent airmen.

'We shall arrive at the first roadblock in the Land Rover at 14.10. The Land Rover will be concealed in the woods here, and we shall put out signs here and here, warning of a vehicle check ahead.' (The floor and a few coins serve to illustrate points. Alternatively the inside roof of the tent and a piece of chalk come in handy.) 'The first four men will cross the road and take up positions here, to deal with any hostile activity. When a vehicle arrives here, two men will go forward to check the vehicle. If there is any reason to be suspicious, ask the occupants to leave the vehicle. If you want a suitcase opened for a search, ask the owner to open it. Do not try to open it yourself. That way you will soon get an indication of whether its contents are safe or dangerous. If a car tries to break through the checkpoint without being stopped, the men in this area will open fire. Nobody is permitted to open fire at any target in this area because we do not want to cause ourselves any casualties. If an enemy armoured vehicle arrives we will not engage it with our rifles, but will report it to HQ. If I am incapacitated my second in command will be . . . ' And so on.

A briefing like this can take half an hour, and you pray that you have left nothing out, and that you have been moderately convincing. At the end of the briefing, as after every task at Cranwell, there comes an unusual component in any training scheme. Before anybody assesses you, your instructor invites you to assess yourself. 'First, Student Officer Mason, how do you think that briefing went?'

'I felt I managed most of it clearly and with confidence, sir, but I got slightly lost in the middle and I completely failed to get the point across about . . . '

'Yes, I agree, and you rambled on far too much about how you were going to deal with any prisoners you took. Did you feel you managed to keep the flight's attention through the middle part of the briefing? No? Nor did I. Does anybody else have any observations?'

By the time your shortcomings and inadequacies have been exposed, by yourself, by your flight commander, and by your fellow students, in the course of the two weeks of these camps, you will know, as they will, whether you have sufficient confidence to command as a Royal Air Force officer. And when you have raced round the countryside leading exercises through smoke and thunderflashes, capturing objectives and defending tactical targets, you will know whether you can apply that confidence to practical effect.

After the second camp, some of the work back at Cranwell comes as a welcome relief. Much of it is in the form of war-gaming, in which you take roles in Operation VALIANT GUARD, and later in Operation VALIANT WARRIOR, a synthesis of your advanced ground defence studies. You have studied modern war-fare and nuclear policy, and now, in the ground defence centre, you gain some idea of how modern warfare develops, and how you might one day play a role in dealing with it. Stronger candidates take command roles in these exercises, to test their talents and prove their potential to the full. Some of the weaker ones benefit greatly from being given serious responsibilities, and many a doubtful career has been rescued by tasks well performed in the defence centre. Studying how to carry out a command role in a war might be acknowledged as relevant by the potential senior officer, even by the future fighter pilot.

But you may bet that no aspiring fighter pilot ever visualised himself going through the next part of the training course, which is known by the unprepossessing title of 'office simulator'. In four and a half days in the office simulator, the student officer faces a comprehensive range of the problems that confront the average station commander. Her Majesty's services, necessarily, float downstream on a raft of set procedures, files, forms, and formality, all designed to enable the officer to cope with the full range of problems according to the book, while at the same time taking into account the vagaries of human nature and presenting him with hazards which he would never have foreseen. Lurking in the outer offices of the simulator block, while you are in charge of the 'station', are a number of officer instructors, who launch at you, usually by telephone, a series of problems designed to test your knowledge of standard operating procedures (SOPs) and your capacity for management. Their side of the telephone conversation is strictly established. Your response depends on you.

'This is Sergeant Smith at the guardroom, sir. The sergeant who is meant to be here has gone off into town to do some shopping, and I'm supposed to go off duty. I wonder what I should do about it?'

The wise officer might suggest that he will call back, giving himself time to look up the SOP. He might even have another task on in hand already, such as hearing a charge against an aircraftman accused of a misdemeanour. Some junior officers can find themselves sitting in judgement like a magistrate within weeks of graduating from Cranwell. Fighter pilots might occupy this unexpected seat rather later in their careers, but they still have to learn how to do it.

'March in the prisoner. Do you understand your rights as a prisoner? What is the charge against him? You have heard what has been said against you. Do you want to ask any questions about that evidence? What do you have to say in answer to the charge? Three days' restrictions. March the prisoner out . . . '

And at the end, the inevitable self-assessment. What did you think of the way you handled that charge? Did you have the prisoner stand in the right place? No, he was too close, and might have been able to take a swing at you. Did you let him go on for too long with irrelevant excuses? Did you think that the punishment was appropriate for the offence? Has anybody else any observations? No? I thought you handled that quite well.

Phew!

Where has all this led? At the end of the course, you will have a range of skills and knowledge that you never thought you would need. You will be fit, confident, and self-possessed, and your flight will show the cohesion and cheerful demeanour of any group of people who have come through a long and intense trial together. You will know how to march and how to handle weapons. You will know how to manage and handle people. You will know how to communicate effectively, in speech and in writing. You will have learned to look after yourself, and solve tricky problems under pressure, with flexibility and leadership. You will know how to run an office, and a war-room, and even a war. You will have taken exams to prove all of this, but more importantly, you will have survived your own ruthless self-assessment at every stage in the process, and will have learned to cope with the honest and sometimes brutal assessment of your peers and instructors.

If you have not performed up to scratch, you might be sent back to cover part of the course again, or even go back over the whole course. All this you will find out on 'black Tuesday', in the seventeenth week of the course, when your postings arrive.

For the record, about 86 per cent pass, out of the 1,200 or so student officers who start on the course. Those 1,200 go through Cranwell in eight courses per year, with 150 cadets on each course. Ten per cent of students are Women's Royal Air Force, and they go through the same syllabus and the same challenges. Some of them come back to Cranwell as flight commanders, instructor-officers looking after new students.

If at any stage in the course there are doubts about whether you are going to make it, there is an elaborate procedure to make sure you are given a fair hearing, and every chance to remedy your deficiencies. Ultimately your case goes before the commanding officer, who has the final say on whether you stay or go.

If 'black Tuesday' turns out to favour you, you can look forward to the formal dinner at the end of the course, and to the passing out parade, at which you become a commissioned officer in the Royal Air Force. If you have GD(P) after your name, you will be able to go on to what you were looking forward to in the first place – General Duties, Pilot. You might not even feel like going away on leave, so anxious are you to get your hands on an aeroplane. But be patient. You are an officer, and your introduction to Royal Air Force flying is now not far away.

# 4

## Building Blocks in the Air

There are several routes by which a student pilot can start on Royal Air Force flying training. Whichever route you take, your introduction to flying will almost certainly be on a light, single-engined, piston-powered aeroplane.

Today, many Royal Air Force entrants are university graduates, and one of the best introductions to military flying is the university air squadron. At fifteen universities up and down Britain, students are having the time of their lives, learning to fly, to military standards, for nothing. Free. Some university air squadron members have already been accepted for the Royal Air Force, and are studying on Royal Air Force Cadetships. They have priority. Any remaining places in the squadron are open to all students to try for. But the competition is fierce. You will have to convince the squadron commander that you have a genuine interest in aviation, and would be an enthusiastic, valuable member of his squadron. There are no commitments. You do not even have to undertake to apply to join the Royal Air Force. And the subject you are reading is irrelevant. If the squadron leader accepts you, you can look forward to two years of flying training, in some of the best flying clubs in the country.

You will learn on the Bulldog. The Bulldog is a sturdy little side-by-side two-seat aeroplane, and definitely on the sporty side for the new student.

The first, simple, fundamental activity – the foundation of all kinds of flying training – is the circuit. In the early stages of his training the student flies circuits *ad nauseam*. If he can fly circuits, he can handle most of the critical parts of flying. When he has shown that he is capable of flying the aeroplane on his own, he will be sent solo, and his first venture in the air alone will be a

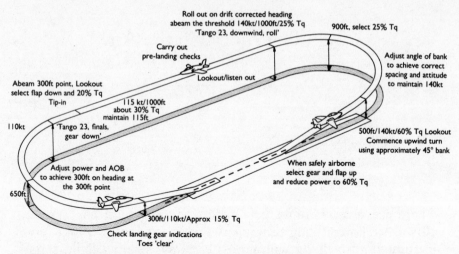

Roll out on drift corrected heading
abeam the threshold 140kt/1000ft/25% Tq
'Tango 23, downwind, roll'

900ft, select 25% Tq

Carry out
pre-landing checks

Adjust angle of bank
to achieve correct
spacing and attitude
to maintain 140kt

Abeam 300ft point, Lookout
select flap down and 20% Tq
Tip-in

Lookout/listen out

115 kt/1000ft
about 30% Tq
maintain 115ft

110kt

'Tango 23, finals,
gear down'

500ft/140kt/60% Tq Lookout
Commence upwind turn
using approximately 45° bank

Adjust power and AOB
to achieve 300ft on heading at
the 300ft point

When safely airborne
select gear and flap up
and reduce power to 60% Tq

650ft

300ft/110kt/Approx 15% Tq

Check landing gear indications
Toes 'clear'

*Fig. 1* The military pilot's oval circuit – exhilarating but busy

circuit. If at any time he gets out of practice, his instructor will take him for a check ride, then send him out to practise circuits.

The circuit is a simple concept. Sign out the aeroplane, carry out the pre-flight checks, strap in, start up, radio for traffic information and clearance for your detail, taxi to the threshold, take off, fly an oval pattern at a specified height with the runway in sight, approach, and land. To achieve a reasonable number of circuits in the course of a lesson, you can let the aeroplane continue to roll down the runway after landing, apply full power, and take off again for another circuit. It saves time taxiing from the end of the runway back to the threshold. Touch and go, it is called, or, alternatively, a roller. Some people, incorrectly, but for many pilots all too accurately, call this training circuits and bumps.

First, you must carry out the pre-flight checks. The pilot, even if he is only a student, and whether he is solo or has an instructor with him, is responsible for the aeroplane, and is obliged to carry out the checks personally to ensure that the aeroplane is fit and safe to fly. There are, in the course of a complete flight, several dozen items which the pilot must check, outside the aircraft on the ground, inside the cockpit before starting up, after start-up, before take-off, immediately after take-off, at several points during the flight, certainly during an emergency, on approach to the airfield, during the penultimate leg of the circuit, on the final approach to land, after landing, and while closing down the aeroplane.

The checks for each type of aircraft are listed in a handy little booklet known as the flight reference cards, or more commonly the check-list. In civilian flying, pilots are expected to learn only those checks which have to be carried out in critical phases of a flight, such as emergencies or on the downwind leg. The remainder, almost all flying schools insist, should be read systematically from a check-list, to ensure that nothing is omitted. Military students have a harder time, and are expected to learn virtually all the checks. There are no shortcuts. You simply have to master them, except, ironically, those which apply in emergencies. For those you retrieve your flight reference cards from the leg pocket of your flying suit, flip it open with the thumb of one gloved hand, and read off the required actions.

Some students have a hard job learning the list well enough to rely on their memory. Each successive Royal Air Force flying school provides a cardboard mockup of its aircraft cockpit, and the student can take it back to the mess, sit in his room, and run through the checks until they are imprinted indelibly in his memory. Some schools also keep an inoperative aeroplane tucked away in the corner of a hangar, usually an old fuselage with no wings, where the student can sit, quietly familiarising himself with the controls and instruments and running through the checks, over and over again.

Let's go flying. First, into the seat. Stand on it if you need to, then slide your legs under the panel. Wriggle your bottom into the seat and make yourself comfortable. Adjust the pedals: a small clip over your toe frees the pedal, and you push it forwards to a comfortable position. Now the parachute straps. In the Bulldog the parachute is in place on the seat. Pull the parachute locking mechanism across your midriff. Pull up the loop between your legs. Draw up the strap from one side, pass it through the loop, and slot it into the locking mechanism. Now the same with the opposite strap. And your shoulder straps. Your ground crew helper will pass them to you over your shoulders, one at a time. Slot them home into the locking mechanism. There are four reassuring clunks. That has strapped the parachute to you. Now strap yourself to the aeroplane. First the main strap between your legs. Next the straps on either side of your seat. Bring them across your thighs, slot them home, and draw them comfortably tight. They will hold you and the aeroplane together when you are inverted. Now the shoulder straps: bring them one over each shoulder and slot them home into the release mechanism. Now sort out the maze and arrange the straps comfortably around each other. You feel like a trussed chicken. Only your arms are free.

The instructor's voice is calm, reassuring, firm. 'You have learned the parachute drill, but we will run through it as a final check. If I want us to abandon the aeroplane I will say "Abandon the aeroplane." Turn the smaller lower locking mechanism at the bottom. Do not touch the parachute locking mechanism at the top. Climb out of the aeroplane and dive at forty-five degrees down through the gap between the wing and the tailplane. Take hold of the steel parachute release and pull it across your chest. Land with your knees slightly bent and your feet together. I do not anticipate that this will be necessary. As this is an early flight in your course, I will carry out the checks and look after the radio, and when I give you control you can concentrate on the flying aspects of the exercise.'

The instructor's hands move rapidly over the controls and across the instrument panel as he carries out the checks, touching each item as he goes. It is daunting to the novice that he can run through them so accurately and so fast. The instructor signals to the ground crew, who pulls away the chocks, then he advances the throttle and the aeroplane sets off at a smart pace out of dispersal.

'I'd like you to taxi out along the yellow line, to the end, turn to the right, and follow the taxiway round to the holding point for Runway One Eight. You have control.'

'I have control, sir.'

It is an exaggeration. The Bulldog has sensitive nosewheel steering. Press with the right foot to bring it back on to the yellow line. It veers across the line. Hit the left pedal and the aeroplane veers back. Too much. Apply less pressure and nothing happens. More pressure, and too much happens, sending us oscillating down the taxiway swinging wildly from side to side. It is a relief when the instructor asks me to turn towards wind for the power checks. I still have control, so until I hear otherwise I am obliged to carry on with the power checks myself. They are in the memory somewhere. It is a question of finding them. Miraculously they appear, and I run through them faultlessly. Then I continue to taxi, with the aeroplane set up for the take-off, and announce my readiness at the holding point.

'Zero Seven ready for departure.'

'Zero Seven clear take-off.'

'Clear take-off, Zero Seven.'

Life is now simple. Turn the aeroplane on to the runway with your toes, trust that your instructor has checked every move you have made, and push the throttle forwards. All the way forwards, for full power. A good steady three-second push. Don't slam it. One and two and three.

The Bulldog accelerates like a sports car, and I try to watch the speed and the runway at the same time. This is one of the phases of flight where the student pilot realises he needs one of flying's greatest skills – the ability to have eyes in two or three different places at once, to know where those places are, and to know what to look for. Forty knots comes up. The Bulldog is turning resolutely left. Apply right rudder; a good bootful, but be careful to keep the toes low to avoid touching the toe brake. That could be embarrassing. Fifty knots; ease the stick firmly back to lift the nosewheel off the concrete. Hold it there. Sixty knots, and the aeroplane rises smoothly into the air. We are flying.

Now, forward on the stick to hold this attitude. If I continue to pull back the nose will come up and the aircraft will stall. Look out of the cockpit to check the horizon. Look into the cockpit to check speed. The best rate-of-climb speed is 80 knots. Once established in the climb, ease the flap switch forward to raise the flaps. The nose drops a fraction, and the speed begins to rise. Raise the nose. Trim the aircraft. Now things begin to happen at headlong speed, and the workload goes up to match.

At 500 ft look out to check around us. We should still be on the heading on which we took off. Never mind if we are not. I can sort that out later. Start the turn. Roll on 20 degrees of bank. Watch the speed. Watch the height. Keep the turn going. Not too much bank. I need to look for 800 ft at 80 knots as I complete the turn. Level the wings. Lower the nose. Look out at the runway on our right. Now, very decisively, pull back the throttle to set the power at 16 in. of manifold pressure. Pull it quite a long way back. There is a lot of throttle movement in this aeroplane. That should give a circuit speed of 80 knots. Now I am losing height. Raise the nose. Add a touch of power or the speed will drop. Not too much.

The runway should now be running along between the roundel and the red/white paint boundary on the Bulldog's wing, if I have flown us the correct distance from the runway, and provided that our wings are level. I try to manoeuvre the aeroplane into the right position and attitude, and give it too much attention. Watch the speed.

And probably the wind will not be precisely down the runway, so I need to correct for drift. The wind was from the left of the runway on take-off. So on this right-hand circuit, point the nose towards the runway. Good. That has stopped the drift. But I need to stop myself admiring my flying. There is work to be done. First the downwind call.

'Zero Seven downwind, to roll.'

'Zero Seven report finals.'

'Zero Seven.'

Now the downwind checks. They come in various forms, depending on the aeroplane, and even on the instructor. But you need to know the essentials, off by heart. Check *fuel*: booster pump on, enough in the tank in use to complete the landing. Check *flaps*, up at this stage, as required. Check *altimeter*: on the QFE setting in the circuit. Check *brakes*; parking brake off; toe brakes show pressure. Apply *carburettor* heat.

By this time we have shot along the downwind leg past the end of the runway, and it is time to start thinking about turning finals. This is one area where military flying differs from its counterpart in civilian flying clubs. In private flying, you extend the downwind leg way beyond the runway threshold, put in a 90-degree turn, fly a good long base leg while you get yourself set up for the approach, wait until you are almost level with the extended centreline of the runway, turn towards it, and fly steadily in for a landing, adjusting your height and maintaining the correct speed. It is a relaxed, leisurely, rectangular circuit, leaving plenty of time at each stage, and affording a margin of safety for even the most unskilled pilot.

The military circuit is not like that at all. It is brisk, highly pressured, and expeditious. You are probably lower than most civilian circuits, which might be flown at anything up to 1,200 ft, depending on the aerodrome rules. The military circuit is unlikely to be flown at anything above 800 ft. And it is not an extended rectangle. You turn finals not off a base leg, but off the downwind leg. The finals leg is fast, beautiful, and exciting – an elegantly curved approach down to a point not far short of the threshold. It is the student pilot's first introduction to anything like the curved approaches that advanced pilots fly on to aircraft carriers. And fun!

First, as we come level with the end of the runway on the downwind leg, pick a point where you anticipate being at 400 ft. If you know the airfield, you will have a feature in your mind for each runway, in each direction, like that farmhouse in the trees, the small lake, or that bridge over the road. At an unfamiliar airfield, look out of the cockpit at 45 degrees as you come level with the threshold. In your mind's eye extend the runway centre-line. Where those two lines cross is going to be your 400-ft point. You are going to fly a well-judged descending turn to arrive overhead that point, at 400 ft.

Instructors have a variety of devices to help you get to that point. One recommended that his students visualise a ribbon of air, rising straight from the end of the runway and curving elegantly to the point where you are now. Just fly down that ribbon of air. Another visualises a doughnut in the sky, over the 400-ft point. All you have to do is fly through the hole in the doughnut.

If you have concentrated on flying the aeroplane accurately during the downwind leg, you should still be at precisely 800 ft, and at 80 knots, as you make the finals turn. If you are not, you will have to make some adjustments as you descend, and your instructor will be having a word with you about it later.

So, ease back the throttle to give 2,200 rpm, which will reduce the speed to 70 knots, and start the descending turn. Lower the nose. Check the height. You should arrive half-way round the turn at 600 ft. If not, throttle forward for a bit more power to slow the rate of descent. Or lower the nose a bit more. Trim the aircraft. Keep it in balance.

Now call finals. 'Zero Seven finals to roll.'

'Zero Seven cleared to roll. Wind 150, fifteen knots.'

'Zero Seven.'

I struggle to lodge that information somewhere in my brain, but it drifts away as I work to manage the rapidly changing picture outside. We have gone through 600 ft more or less half-way through the turn, and we are approaching 400 ft, but short of the extended centreline. Open out the turn a bit. The trouble with flying is that there is no time to stop to make any corrections. It all happens on the wing. While I am still trying to get the height right, the 400-ft point that I was aiming for has disappeared somewhere beneath me. Only the runway has any relevance now.

One of the most interminably debated topics in all of aviation centres on how you use the throttle and control column to maintain your glide slope and airspeed on the final approach. No two experts will agree on the more sophisticated aspects of the equation, but in simple terms, traditional teaching, both civilian and military, has adopted the philosophy that you use throttle to adjust your rate of descent, and attitude to adjust your speed.

If you are too high, reduce the power. You will lose thrust, and your descent will take you lower for a given distance flown over the ground. You will also lose lift, so you will tend to descend faster. Altogether you will get back on to the correct glide-slope. The opposite is also true. If you are too low advance the throttle to put on the power, and you will gain thrust and lift, getting back on to the correct glide-slope.

Obviously, reducing power to stop yourself being too high also reduces your speed, and as speed is one of the most important elements in the landing, you need to lower the nose to maintain the correct speed. Conversely, adding power when you are too low will give you lift, but can reduce your airspeed, so you may need to lower the nose to regain the required speed. As with everything else in flying, there are infinite numbers of other complications, but at the level of basic simplicity, that has been the traditional story. Power controls your rate of descent. Elevator, through the control column, controls airspeed.

The Royal Air Force has turned that upside down. Not all flying instructors, especially the more mature ones steeped in the traditions of perfectionist flying, agree, but the message is now simple. It has been designed to prepare pilots for the practice that they will adopt later when they come on to fast-jet flying. The rule is: point the aircraft at the spot on the runway where you want to land, and use the throttle to adjust the speed. Simple.

That is the philosophy, but we have no more than seconds to sort it out in the air. We are on final approach, full flap set. I have my feet on the rudder pedals to maintain a balanced aircraft; toes off the toe-brakes. Point the aircraft at the skid marks just the other side of the piano keys, where I want to land.

'Speed too high. Seventy knots is your speed.'

I risk a glance at the airspeed indicator: 72 knots. Back a little on the throttle. He is being very precise.

'Not quite on the centreline. Try to land your cockpit on the centreline. Forget where the nose of the aircraft is. Use that map-clip as the foresight; your bum as the rear-sight. Aim the aeroplane. Speed too low.'

Another glance at the ASI: 69 knots. Hardly a wide margin off the ideal, but he is looking for perfection today. Touch of power if he says so. I am still pointing the aeroplane. And the runway is coming up to meet us. I seem to be diving head-first to meet it. The temptation is to pull the stick back to avoid a splintering contact. Forget about the centreline. We are nearly there and there is no time to adjust anything any more. Just hold it.

'Fly it right down to the runway.'

I force myself to keep it going down the hill, fighting the temptation to pull back. Then the runway is there. I must pull back on the stick now. It is the key to all standard landings, the essence of all the early training. The round-out, it is called. And this entire phase of the landing is called the flare. Flown correctly, it is a beautiful, gentle manoeuvre, a graceful climax to your flight. Flown with the slightest error, and you look and feel like the most incompetent hamfisted choppable student who ever climbed into an aeroplane. If you flare too late the aeroplane will hit the concrete and bounce, then descend and bounce again. Flare too early and it will balloon into the air, and you will find yourself bringing it down again a third of the way along the runway, or it will stall at too great a height because you lost flying speed, and it will crunch down on to the runway with a metal-bending thump. The 'window' between the height where you round out far too early and bang into the runway, and the height at which you round out too late and bounce off the runway, is narrow. And all the time you are controlling the aeroplane with your two hands, and using your feet in the final seconds to keep it straight.

The instructor tries to talk me through it: 'Look along the runway. Flare now. Power off. Keep the aircraft straight. Now stop it landing.'

Everything is set up. You can do nothing else. Just keep it

pointing down the runway with your feet. Pull the stick right back into your stomach as if you wanted it to stay in the air, and the nose will just keep tilting up as the mainwheels squeak gently down to the concrete.

'That was a good landing.'

Elated, you are tempted to throw up your hands and quit for the day while you are ahead. But there is work to be done. This is a touch-and-go.

'Full power then.' He continues to talk me through it. 'Touch of right rudder. Full power! All the way. Stick back at fifty knots to raise the nosewheel, and there she flies off at sixty knots. Hold the nose down to gain your climbing speed of – what?'

'Eighty knots, sir.'

'Good. And when you are established in the climb, flaps to intermediate. Look around. Flaps up, and at five hundred feet begin the turn.'

And off you go on another circuit. Your circuit training goes on . . . standard circuits, low-level circuits, glide approaches, flap-less circuits, each requiring a variation in the technique.

There is one type of approach and landing that hardly qualifies as a circuit, and is nothing like any manoeuvre the private pilot will ever see, at least not at a serious airfield under air traffic control. It is the run in and break, and even in a small primary trainer it has an element of panache and thrill that will send the student's spine tingling. The student can practise it as a variation on the final approach to a landing, or it can be used as a standard join. The run in and break, apart from being a lot of fun, has a serious military purpose.

Start from a point two miles out from the threshold, on the runway extended centreline. Call 'Zero Seven initials.' (Initials is the point where we start the run in.)

Turn off a long downwind leg and aim to arrive at initials at about 800 ft. Apply full power and lower the nose to increase the speed. We are looking for 500 ft, and we can expect to fly the approach at about 145 knots. The Bulldog engine builds up to the deep throaty roar of a quality sports car. The speed builds up to 145 knots, and a sneaky look at the ground shows just how quickly the trees and buildings are flashing by, though there is not much time for sightseeing. At 500 ft level off. I need to aim to arrive just on the dead side of the runway, the side opposite to the circuit side. Then if anybody else should happen to be on finals as I approach, I will not interfere with their circuit, and I will not be in the way of anybody taking off or opting for a go-around.

Hold the height and speed. Trim the aircraft. I am beginning to feel the thrill at the back of the neck. This is the run in. Now, just past the threshold, turn in with a brisk banking manoeuvre. Cross the runway over to the circuit side. Maintain full power and climb, up towards circuit height. That is the break – a sharp decisive scything climbing turn from the safety of the dead side into the busy circuit, where we need to watch for other aircraft. In seconds, the aircraft intercepts the curving line that would have been the final approach of an orthodox circuit. So keep the turn going, right round in a tight little circle. Check fuel, flaps, altimeter, brakes. And maintain the descent to arrive at the threshold for a landing. Power back to give 70 knots. Trim. Intermediate flap. Call finals and declare intentions. Acknowledge permission to land. Full flap. Hold on the bank and pitch to maintain the descending turn. Keep the power adjusted to maintain 70 knots. Keep looking out, and keep monitoring the instruments at the same time. Fly down the ribbon of air to line up just before the threshold. Keep one eye on the airspeed, the other on the runway. Keep the descent going. Flare the aircraft, and land. Brilliant.

The run in and break is a manoeuvre designed for war, when an aircraft returning to base will not have time for a standard join and a long grind round the orthodox circuit, even the abbreviated oval military one. There are even more refinements in the world of fast jets, where the run in can be as low as 200 ft, then break, and power off, airbrake out, turn and climb, and join the circuit for a tight turn, gear and flaps, and in to a landing, with all the landing checks and calls packed into that.

Then there is the formation run in and break, practised by slightly more advanced students. The run in is in echelon, two or three or four aeroplanes one behind the other. All on the same radio frequency, they run in until the leader is abeam the threshold. Then each announces his break in turn.

'Number One break,' and he pulls away into his circle.

Wait five seconds . . . two, three, four . . . 'Number Two break.'

Then, two, three, four, 'Number Three break.' And they pull round in a well-formed turn to complete the approach to a precise, pretty, sequential landing.

The hours build up, and circuit consolidation begins to form a major element in training. Round and round, lesson after lesson, dual until the instructor has satisfied himself that you are flying the aeroplanes in the prescribed manner, then solo, to build your confidence.

Even in these early stages, you begin to see where the requirements of military flying diverge from those of its civilian equivalent. Driving an aeroplane round the skies is not the way the fighter pilot is going to spend most of his time. At this stage, nobody has any idea which of the trainees will make fast-jet pilots, which of them multi-engined, and which rotary-wing. So all go through the same process, to teach them to fly the aircraft to the limits of its performance. And that means aerobatics. Many a student finds that he is learning aerobatics before he has even gone solo. If the weather is not good enough for the instructor to send a student solo, he can still take him above the clouds for off-circuit training.

It is probably inaccurate, or at least unusual, to describe the spin as an advanced aerobatic manoeuvre, as one Chief Flying Instructor (CFI) did. But learning it does let you know how comfortably you are going to take to three-dimensional flying in fighter aircraft. Civilian students are no longer subjected to the dramas of the fully developed spin. They are taught merely to recognise the symptoms of an incipient spin, and to prevent the spin developing. Military pilots, who will later fly their aircraft in complex manoeuvres, risk putting the aircraft into an unintentional spin many times in the course of a combat sortie, and need to learn how to recover from it. The only way is to rehearse recovery from an intentional spin. The lesson follows the customary pattern, with an extended briefing on the white board, and much use of coloured pens.

'Aim: the aim is to recognise the spin, and to enter and recover with minimum height loss.

'Airmanship: you have learned the HASELL checks, and we will carry out a full 360-degree turn to ensure that our airspace is clear.' You rack your brain to remember the sequence of checks – Height, Airframe, Security, Engine, Location, Lookout – for which HASELL is the mnemonic.

'Air Exercise: the entry is the same as the stall. But at 60 knots, apply full rudder in the direction you wish to spin. Pull the control column fully back. We shall use both hands on the control column. Hold the controls there. The symptoms are: low and stable indicated airspeed. The vertical speed indicator will be fully down. The turn needle will be fully to the left or to the right.

'Now recovery. I will enter the first spin. For the recovery, which I will show you. I shall say "Recovering Now." What do you think would be the correct action to minimise height loss? Yes. Power off. Now to stop the spin check the turn needle and determine which way you are spinning. Apply full opposite rudder. Move the control column fully forward. When the spin stops, centralise the rudder. Look out of the cockpit at the horizon. Level the wings, and ease out of the dive.'

After the fronts of the day before, the weather is improving. There are holes in the cumulus, and we can fly up through them towards the patches of blue overhead. A few miles to the west a band of clear air is approaching, but on this last day of November there is no time to wait for perfect weather. We have to stick to our allotted slot in the busy flying schedule, and if we delay we might be out in the dark. Somewhere above 6,000 ft we break out of the clouds into brilliant sunshine with a deep blue sky. The cumulus marches away below us in an expanse of towering peaks, until it suddenly stops, and I feel I want to take the aeroplane over there and play on the other side. But it is pleasant enough here, so we climb in a steady droning spiral, meeting the dazzling sun head-on every 360 degrees. If I put the sun visor on my helmet up I can see nothing. If I lower it, I can see outside the aeroplane, but I can see nothing on the instrument panel down in the dark of the cockpit in front of me. 'Try your visor half-way,' the instructor suggests helpfully. It works, and I can see the magic of the skyscape and monitor the instruments at the same time. But even here there is no chance to enjoy the moment. There is work to be done, starting with some arithmetic, performed, mercifully in this first lesson, by the CFI on his kneepad.

'What height do we need for the spin? If we have to abandon the aeroplane we must do so by the transition level of 4,000 ft, plus 300 ft for the ground, rounded to 4,500 ft. Add 3,500 ft for the height at which we must start our recovery from an intentional spin. Add to that 350 ft for each of four turns. What is four times 350. Yes, 1,400. Round that up to 1,500. Added up that makes 9,500 ft to start the spin. Keep climbing. Keep the airspeed at 80 knots. If you let the nose come up we shall lose airspeed.'

We go on winding up into the cool crystal air, clearing our ears as we go.

'Do you recall the HASELL checks? I will carry out the first ones and you can fly the lookout turn. Height: we need to be at 9,500 ft for the spin. Airframe: flaps are up. Security: check that your straps are tight, doors locked and latched, nothing loose behind you; if you would turn and check behind me, please. Engine: temperatures and pressures in the green, fuel is in balance, induction heat on, booster pump on. Location: well that is Stanford in the Vale I see down there, and that is Farringdon. Keep away from them. Not over a built-up area or active airfield, and not in controlled airspace. And we are in sight of the ground. Aim along the left of that gap in the clouds.

'Now do you recall the recovery actions?'

I try to recall them, with too much hurry: 'Throttle closed. Full opposite rudder.'

He corrects me firmly: 'No, first check the turn needle. Remember you might be in an unintentional spin and you could be misled about the direction of the spin.'

I try again: 'Throttle closed. Check the turn needle. Full opposite rudder. Control column fully forward. And ease out of the dive.'

'Centralise the rudder, then pull out of the dive, looking at the horizon. And remember to say, "Recovering Now." Now we are approaching 9,500 ft, so if you would level off and fly a turn to the left to check that we are clear below . . . not too much bank, and right round to the west, I will show you the first spin.

'Power off. As the airspeed falls to 70 knots, trim the aeroplane and check that the trim indicator is in the take-off band. Both hands on the control column, stick fully back, and at 60 knots full left rudder.'

I have always thought that you can assess pilots quite simply by their reactions to the entry into a spin. If they like it, they will make pilots. If they are terrified, they probably won't make pilots. I think I am still a little bit frightened by it. From inside the cockpit, it looks utterly, totally, terrifyingly dramatic. First, the left wing disappears, as the aircraft rolls violently, almost on to its back. An instant afterwards the nose pitches down, and the aircraft seems to be in a screaming inverted dive. An instant after that yaw becomes apparent, and together these three motions – roll, pitch, and yaw – the classic elements of a fully developed spin, sort themselves out and the aircraft stabilises into a smooth nose-down twisting motion.

The instructor is totally unperturbed. 'You see the airspeed has dropped off the clock. Vertical speed is right at the bottom. Turn needle is fully left.'

I try to follow his calm hypnotic voice, but there are stronger forces working in my brain. One is the ground below, which is a deep dark shade of grey in shadow from the surrounding cloud. And it is revolving. And I am heading straight down to corkscrew into it. I risk a look out of the windscreen, and find that the horizon is only just above eye level, so we must be in a fairly shallow nose-down attitude. Confusion and disorientation are endemic among student pilots in early spin training.

'So, recovering now. Throttle closed. Check turn needle. It is left, so full right rudder. Stick fully forward. Spin stops. Centralise rudder. Ease out of the dive. Throttle fully forward with a gentle push. Look at the horizon. Wings level and climb away. You see we have lost 1,400 ft. You have control. For the next spin I'd like you to fly the entry, then I'll take control and recover. Then you can fly the entry and recovery.'

Climbing back to 9,500 ft takes another eternity. It leaves me plenty of time to rehearse the checks, and plenty of time to get nervous and worried and depressed about my coming performance. The entry is as dramatic as ever, the instructor's recovery as correct, the climb back as interminable. Now it is my turn for the full entry and recovery. The checks are abbreviated after the first spin, to HELL checks. Height: 9,500 ft. Engine. Location: the instructor is satisfied that he knows where we are. And Lookout: fly a full 360-degree turn to look out below and all round. Roll out on a westerly heading. Nothing for it now. We are committed. Power off; 70 knots. Trim to the take-off range. Both hands on the stick. Stick fully back; 60 knots. Oh, Christ! Full left rudder. *Wham.* The wing drops. The aeroplane rolls, dives, turns, settles. And revolves . . . revolves . . . revolves. Check the turn needle.

'Recover now,' he says firmly.

Full right rudder. Stick forward. Spin stops. We seem to be in a screaming vertical dive. Pull back on the stick. The g forces come on, tugging at the arms.

'Centralise rudder,' he orders.

The sky is in front of us.

'Now full power, slowly. Watch the speed. Stick forward now or we'll stall.'

I know I made a hash of it.

'Like to try another. OK. Remember. First close the throttle. Then check the turn needle. Full opposite rudder. Stick firmly forward. When the spin stops centralise the rudder, and stick back to ease out of the dive. Power on and wings level to climb away.'

By my count that is six key actions, and I try to implant them in the memory. Power off. Turn needle. Full opposite rudder. Stick forward. Centralise rudder. Fly out. If I get through those six actions in the course of a spin and emerge unscathed I shall feel I am getting the hang of it. So back to 9,500 ft, and complete the HELL checks. Fly a full turn. Close the throttle. Stick back with two hands. And as she slows, full right rudder. *Wham*. Over. Even that is becoming less of an ordeal now that I know that it is going to stabilise into a relatively gentle spin. Round, and round, and round.

'Recover now.'

Check throttle closed. Look at the turn needle. At least I remembered that. It is hard over to the right. Full left rudder. Stick fully forwards. Spin stops. Stick back.

'Centralise rudder.' (Did he think I was forgetting it?)

Centralise rudder. Stick back. There is the sky dead ahead.

'Throttle slowly forward.'

I climb out and back up to 9,500 ft. By the end of the fifth spin of the sortie I seem to be getting the hang of it, and even seem to be getting a taste for the spin.

'That was fine,' as we make our way back in the gathering dusk. 'You were improving at a good average rate for a competent student. I would like to hear you say "Recovering Now" as you begin your recovery actions, so that I know your intentions.'

'Yes, sir.'

I resolve to make sure that I know the checks, and have rehearsed and re-rehearsed the actions for the spin and the recovery until they are indelibly fixed in my memory. Next time I must be able to do it perfectly. After all I shall soon have to convince the instructor that I can perform the spin solo. And before long I shall have to enter the spin as the climax to some aerobatic manoeuvre such as a roll off the top. And one day, perhaps – this being, after all, one of the main purposes of spin training – I might have to recover from a wholly unintentional spin. I must learn and master the sequence of actions, until I can carry them out as convincingly and as unhurriedly as he can.

# 5

## The Chipmunk Route

In parallel with the university students, who have a relatively unpressured two years to get as far ahead in the flying syllabus as their time and enthusiasm allow, another group is approaching an identical goal from a totally different direction: direct entrants to the Royal Air Force. They might be any age from seventeen, the youngest that an officer candidate can be accepted, to twenty-three, the oldest that he can be accepted for aircrew training. Most of them have no previous flying experience. They might be university graduates, who did not have the opportunity or desire to fly with a university air squadron, or recent school leavers anxious to avoid loitering in university before starting a service career. They are all commissioned officers in the Royal Air Force, with their eighteen-week course of initial officer training at RAF Cranwell behind them, and the single stripe of a pilot officer on their flying suits. These are student pilots at the Elementary Flying Training School (EFTS), at RAF Swinderby in Lincolnshire. They have just sixteen weeks in which to complete their elementary flying training, which amounts to sixty-five hours and fifteen minutes' flying, plus ground school and exams. They are learning to fly in Chipmunks. Theirs in many ways is the toughest of the options.

Students who learn to fly with the university air squadrons rarely suffer the indignity of the chop. If things are not going well they have plenty of time to sort out the difficulties, and they can pace themselves through the course. They may learn early on that they are not going to make the grade as fast-jet pilots, but that does not remove them from the squadron, and within reason they can go on enjoying their flying lessons, however unsuited they may be to flying as a profession, right up to the end of the course.

At EFTS, by contrast, the student is pitched in, raw and

untutored, to the stresses of military flying. He must perform. EFTS used to be called FSS, the Flying Selection School. The purpose behind that name still lingers, and the instructors know that they are in the business not only of teaching the elements of flying, but of deciding who has the aptitude and who does not. There is very little flexibility to wait for an improvement. Tests at points along the way show whether the student has the capacity and ability to fly. If not, he goes on review. He gets a new instructor, two hours of extra tuition, and a repeat of the test. If he still proves unsuitable, he goes in front of the commanding officer to discuss alternative non-flying opportunities in the Royal Air Force, or to consider whether he wants to remain in the service at all.

The Chipmunk, as any pilot who has flown it will tell you, is a delightful little aeroplane, but a rascal if you fail to control it. Designed in the 1940s, and first in service in the 1950s, it has the feel of a vintage aeroplane and the smell of pioneer flying. It is a tandem-seat aeroplane, with the student in the front and the instructor in the back, so it finds favour with today's service philosophy. It is also a tailwheel aeroplane, colloquially known as a tail dragger, though that term dismisses unfairly the exquisite precision needed to fly it correctly.

'This is raw flying,' my instructor assured me in an early sortie. 'Fly the Chipmunk and you can fly anything.'

Some instructors, especially younger ones, and even the younger ones at EFTS, do not much hold with the Chipmunk system, especially as a means of selecting the natural aviators from the rest. How, they argue, can you use the ability to perform a perfect three-point landing, and to take off or land a skittish aeroplane without ground-looping it, as a guide to a young man's ability to fly and operate a modern fighter, in which computers do a lot of the flying, and the pilot selects weapons and operates their delivery systems? The traditionalists dismiss such heresies, and they still have the day. The aspiring Tornado or EFA (European Fighter Aircraft) pilot hones his skills on an aeroplane that would have been familiar to his grandfather training to fly Spitfires for the Battle of Britain.

It so happens that when you hear a couple of Chipmunks start their engines you are reminded of the evocative throaty roar of the Merlin-engined Spitfire. Instructors would dearly love just a fraction of the Spitfire's muscle in the distinctly under-powered Chipmunk, but they cannot have everything. What they do have is an aeroplane that has charm, guts, character, and almost a mind of its own. It is an aeroplane, the instructors insist, that you have to fly all the time. Hence it is an exceptionally good aeroplane on which to sort the fliers from the triers.

The Chipmunk is one of the few aircraft still in service into which you climb wearing your parachute. Strap on the parachute on the tarmac, step on to the wing and climb into the cockpit, guide your parachute cushion into the steel tray that forms your seat, and sit on it. The ground crew will adjust your legroom by sliding the seat forwards or back, following which strapping in is the same as in any other trainer, with thigh and shoulder straps slotted home into the central buckle. Any resemblance to other aircraft ends there. The long Chipmunk nose rises in front of you, obscuring the view. Your pilot's guide warns you to check in front before you strap in, to make sure that there are no obstacles on the apron, because you will not be able to see them from the cockpit.

Starting can take place only with the aid of your ground crew. Hold your two hands in the air so that your ground handler can see you are touching no controls, and he will insert a sheaf of cartridges into the engine. Pull the starter wire with its steel ring, and the engine leaps into life with a bang and an acrid whiff of cordite. Raw flying indeed!

Taxiing out, I find it disconcerting to be able to see nothing directly ahead. I have to swing the aircraft from side to side to check forwards by peering round the edge of the cowling. Even that is by no means easy, and the Chipmunk is notorious for its difficulty in steering on the ground, at least for the novice pilot. The reason is a hideously complicated system of differential braking, which, in a more sophisticated form, is a familiar system of steering in modern aircraft, where nosewheel steering may not be fitted, or where it is inadequate for the radius of turn required. It simply means that you have to dab the brake on one side only. Dab the left brake with your toe, and the aircraft will turn slightly left, pivoting on the locked wheel. You get used to applying the correct amount of braking, or correcting on the opposite side to compensate, to persuade the aircraft to steer in the desired direction.

Chipmunk students face three problems. One is that you are

eternally over-compensating. To give yourself the view you swing down the taxiway like a car on a skid-pan, never quite sure whether you have control or not. The second is that differential braking is applied by a complicated system involving the handbrake, or parking brake as aviators prefer to call it. Push one rudder forwards all the way with your foot, depress the locking ring on the handbrake, pull the handle back three or four clicks until you feel pressure, then release the locking ring. Your differential braking is now set, and you should be able to taxi. Of course, you do not want any brake at all during your take-off roll or during landing, so you have to release the parking brake altogether when you line up to take off. That releases your differential braking, and you are now totally reliant on steering by means of the rudder itself. The rudder, like other control surfaces, is virtually ineffective at low speeds, so as you start to roll you have little directional control.

Let's try it. Advance the throttle to full power. Release the brakes, and get ready with the feet. The Chipmunk rolls, then veers left as the propeller sends a spiralling current of air along the fuselage and across the fin and rudder. Apply right rudder. Hardly noticeable at first, this becomes more effective as you gain speed. But by now we are pointing off to the right. The only mitigating feature is that as we gain speed, we gain control, so left rudder, and it swings smartly into line, then through the line and across to the left. You need less rudder as the airflow begins to bite.

The opposite will be true on landing, when the speed is reducing all the time, and you have no differential braking. You have to maintain direction by the use of rudder alone. It is almost impossible to keep the aeroplane straight, or to apply the right amounts of correction, and the student in a tailwheel aeroplane who has not ground-looped and found himself suddenly pointing in the wrong direction during his take-off roll, will surely sooner or later find himself in this embarrassing posture after landing.

The speed is building up, so stick forward to lift the tailwheel (that is an unnatural action that I shall have to eradicate on later aeroplanes) and suddenly we are airborne, and all the difficulties with the steering disappear, and the little Chipmunk becomes as responsive and honest an aeroplane as there is. Ask it to do something, and it will do it instantly. Forget to keep it in control, and it will respond to your mistakes, letting you know that you

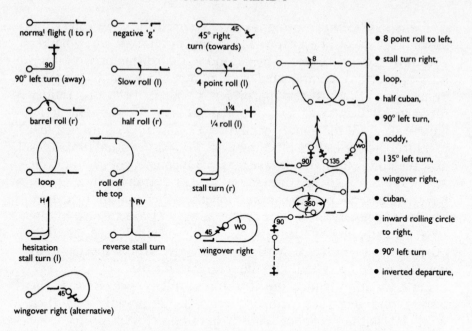

normal flight (l to r)

negative 'g'

45° right turn (towards)

90° left turn (away)

Slow roll (l)

4 point roll (l)

barrel roll (r)

half roll (r)

¼ roll (l)

loop

roll off the top

stall turn (r)

hesitation stall turn (l)

reverse stall turn

wingover right

wingover right (alternative)

- 8 point roll to left,
- stall turn right,
- loop,
- half cuban,
- 90° left turn,
- noddy,
- 135° left turn,
- wingover right,
- cuban,
- inward rolling circle to right,
- 90° left turn
- inverted departure,

*Fig. 2* An aerobatic sequence, built up from linked manoeuvres, and described (*bottom*) by the 'Aresti' symbology

| Loop | Slow roll | 4-point roll | ½ roll | ½ Cuban |
| --- | --- | --- | --- | --- |
| ½ horiz 8 | Roll off the top | ½ Roll-and pull through | Outside stall turn | 90° turn |
| Outside turn | Stall turn | Noddy stall turn | Vertical roll (with stall turn) | Start manoeuvre symbol |
| End manoeuvre symbol | Positive G flight | Negative G flight | Full rolls | Half rolls |

need to pay attention. Even flying straight and level, with 90 knots indicated airspeed and at a fixed height, the slightest lack of attention will let the aircraft climb or descend, and the speed decay or increase accordingly. It is an aeroplane for alert students only.

It is also one of the best aeroplanes in which to learn aerobatics. One of the great joys of any course of training for the military student is that he starts aerobatics at an early stage. It is not a separate activity tacked on after the standard parts of the flying training are completed, but an integral element in the trainee's armoury. Some pilots do not enjoy aerobatics. Some have sensitive stomachs that do not allow them to enjoy aerobatics. The lucky ones have no such qualms, and take easily to the joys of this free-flowing, uninhibited, sometimes weightless, sometimes overweighted three-dimensional expression of the pilot's art. Aerobatic flying is an emotional business. Do it badly and you will feel depressed and incompetent about all your flying. Do it well and you feel like an airborne dolphin, playing freely in time and space, and enjoying mastery over the most sophisticated and complex machines yet invented, the aeroplane.

The aerobatics syllabus is a lengthy catalogue of formal manoeuvres. First, the student learns them individually. Then he learns to string them together, and when the time comes for his test, he will be expected to perform a fluid sequence that will impress the examiner sitting behind him. Loop, aileron roll, slow roll, hesitation roll, flick roll, barrel roll, vertical roll, stall turn, noddy stall turn, roll off the top, half-roll and pull through, clover leaf, Cuban eight, half Cuban, Immelman turn – when you have spent hour after hour learning and rehearsing these, you begin to feel that you really can fly the aeroplane, and you are beginning to develop a genuine understanding of its capabilities.

The point of aerobatics has changed over the years. Almost all aerobatic manoeuvres were designed either to allow the pilot to escape from an enemy who was on his tail, or as an aggressive manoeuvre to put the pilot in an attacking position on the enemy's tail. Learning aerobatics was learning the art of combat manoeuvring. More recently, dogfighting based on aerobatics has been superseded by different forms of combat manoeuvring, designed for that specific purpose in modern fighter aircraft. But aerobatics has remained in the training to give the pilot knowledge of the aeroplane's capabilities, so that he can fly it in combat to its design limits without having to think about it. Instinctive control of the aeroplane through aerobatics training leaves him free to concentrate on getting himself out of danger and putting the enemy aeroplane into it. More recent developments still are taking even that worry out of the pilot's hands, as flight computers calculate for him the optimum way to fly the aircraft. If he wants to go somewhere, the modern pilot in his computer-controlled aircraft only has to apply a demand input with his stick. The aircraft will work out for him the best way to do it. It will not allow him, for example, to exceed the optimum angle of attack or rate of turn. It should prevent him getting into a spin. If he does manage to get into a spin it will probably tell him what to do to regain control.

But students still have to learn to fly, and despite the advance in aerospace technology, aerobatics still has its place. If you can fly aerobatics, you can fly upside down, and on your side, while pulling g or pushing negative g, and you can fly the infinite numbers of transitions between them and still know where you are without becoming disoriented. And once you can do that, when the time comes for you to fly in combat in an infinitely more advanced aircraft, you will be able to manoeuvre with confidence.

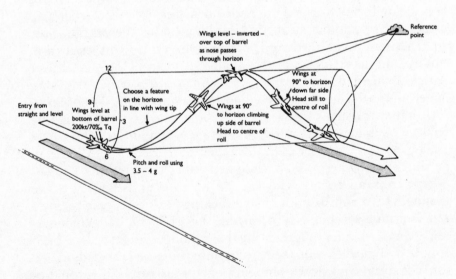

*Fig. 3* The barrel roll, the gentlest but most easily mishandled aerobatic manoeuvre

Of all the standard aerobatic manoeuvres the most difficult to fly in complete control, and the most satisfying to master, must be the barrel roll, which originated during the First World War, when pilots used it to evade an aircraft on their tail. If you have an aircraft directly behind you in a shooting position, you fly a circular manoeuvre round the path of your flight. This slows you down, and you emerge from the manoeuvre back on your original flight path. And because you have slowed down, the enemy aircraft that was on your tail has now overtaken you, and in theory you should now be on his tail, in a perfect firing position.

Before all aerobatics, you need to carry out your HASELL checks. Check your Height. Check that the Airframe is as required with flaps up. Check Security – no loose articles or straps. Check the Engine instruments. Check the Location (ABC is a good mnemonic: not over *Active Airfield*; not over a *Built-up area*, not in *Controlled airspace*). Put in two 180-degree turns to make a good Lookout.

Choose a reference point on or near the distant horizon. Throttle forward to full power, and lower the nose until you have 110 knots. We are barrel rolling to the left, so stick over to dive down to the right. A smooth descending turn. As the airspeed increases to 120 knots, apply pitch. Decisively! Pull up! I want to be still in a right turn, so I need to delay levelling the wings. Now, as the nose starts to come up through the horizon, centre the stick, so that the wings roll level as I fly well into the climb with the nose pointing skywards. Continue to apply aileron, and hold on the pitch. Before long the ground appears from the left, and I get the sensation of flying on a knife-edge, with the wings pointing directly up and down. We should be at the twelve o'clock position in the roll, directly above the original reference point. And there it is. At which point, just when I thought it was going to work, it all falls apart in my hands.

Some instructors make a practice of taking control at this point, when the manoeuvre is half completed. It gets the student used to setting up the roll correctly, and takes the problem of completing it out of his hands. He can establish a pattern of success for the entry phase, and learn how to complete the roll later.

The aeroplane should now start to come through the vertical. After staring straight up at the sky for a second or so, I have a new view of the ground, somewhere off my left front, with the horizon rotating dizzily in front of me. We are still climbing, and rolling toward the inverted position. Now the pitch control becomes less effective. As one instructor put it, you have 'gone ballistic', as the energy stored up in the dive sends us over the top. We are still rolling, using the ailerons, and we should become inverted by the nine o'clock position in the circle. Anybody who has remained genuinely in control until now has a supernatural talent for aerobatics. Mere mortals have to rely on holding the controls roughly steady, and the aeroplane will arrive more or less upright. The correct movement is to relax the pitch for the third quarter of the roll, to prevent the aeroplane from entering a steep inverted dive, and relax the aileron to prevent the aeroplane from flipping upright. Remembering to do all these things, whilst inverted, and whilst the ground is revolving above my head and moving across my field of vision, is impossible.

Time after time I emerge from the barrel roll completely disoriented, and when I rediscover my brains I find myself somewhere near 90 degrees to the direction of entry, and hurtling earthwards. The secret lies in practice, and in setting up the entry perfectly.

'The mistake most students make is to start the roll too early. There, you've just done it yourself,' observes the instructor.

I am not sure whether that is a helpful comment or not. I try to remember his guidance during earlier attempts. Here we go. Dive to the right, then pitch up quite vigorously. Delay the roll, so that the wings come level well after the nose comes up through the horizon. Just wait till I see a canopy full of sky. I work out a system of my own. From now on I shall call it the barrel loop, to remind myself that I have to start the manoeuvre largely as a loop, and take care not to start rolling until the loop is well established. That might help to eradicate my most persistent fault: the shallow entry and the diving exit.

And I try to keep my awareness and control over what is happening, through the manoeuvre. Time after time, usually somewhere inverted, the brain seems to switch off momentarily, like alternating electric current, then switch back on in the other direction, picking up the picture again as we come down the other side. As we go inverted, I struggle manfully to relax the pitch, but I seem to have a fear of letting go an iron grip on the controls. But something seems to be working.

'Well done,' says the voice from the back, as if I knew what I have been doing. 'That was a good one. There's the reference point, above that power station just to the left of the nose, and we have levelled off at our original height.'

I have looped, rolled, merged the two together, and somehow emerged straight and level and in good order. It would be gratifying to think that I had really controlled it, all the way through, but at least an accidentally good roll is better than an accidentally bad roll, so I shall accept the praise, and keep trying to improve. Well performed, the barrel roll is a gently flowing continuous manoeuvre, with no rapid changes of direction and a constant light g force to hold you in the seat.

If it has an opposite, it must be the stall turn, which looks like the peak on a cardiogram read-out, and is probably just as useful as a test of the condition of the heart. The pattern of the stall turn is to fly vertically upwards until the aircraft runs out of energy, turn it through 180 degrees and fly vertically downwards, then

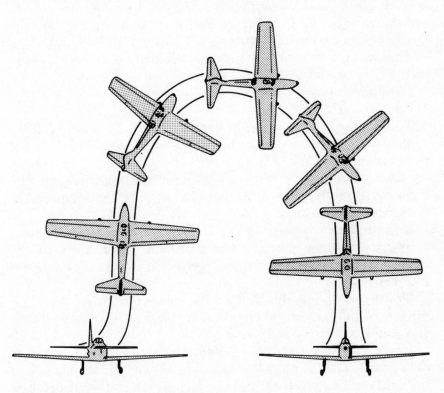

*Fig. 4* The stall turn – easy one way, easily bungled the other

recover into level flight. When you can do that, there are some interesting variations to try. It sounds, like many examples of the aerobatics art, perfectly straightforward, until you start to put the theory into practice and find how many opportunities there are for the theory to break down.

I have carried out the checks, which will cover the whole of this continuous aerobatics session. So I need to fly directly ahead along a line feature, which I am using as a reference, then lower the nose and apply full power to gain speed. Stick back smoothly and firmly and into the climb. Look out along the wing. Aim to straighten out the flight path just short of the vertical. Keep going straight up until the aircraft stops climbing. Now, right rudder. The right wing drops, and falls neatly through the horizon. Next the nose comes round to the right and through the horizon, and now the left wing comes down to the horizon. As the aeroplane's nose points directly towards the ground, centralise the rudder, and centralise the stick. Close the throttle, pull back on the stick to put on some g, and look up. As the nose comes up through the horizon gently ease the throttle to full power and climb out.

That was well executed – elegant and satisfying. It was also the instructor's demonstration.

'You have control.'

'I have control, sir.'

This is the one. It looks easy, compared with the barrel roll, so I shall try to make it work precisely. First the speed. Stick forward to lower the nose and watch for 110 knots. By now I am getting confident enough to give myself a running commentary on the manoeuvre, really to show off that I know what I am supposed to be doing.

'Pull up to nearly vertical. Look along the wing. Stick forward a touch.' It is not enough. The aeroplane comes through the vertical, and as it runs out of energy it falls on to its back. I am completely disoriented.

'Power off. Look up. Pull to the ·nearest horizon. Ease the throttle to full power and climb away.' At least you showed that you could make the correct recovery.

I try again. Speed 110 knots. Pull. This time stop well short of the vertical. The Chipmunk seems to be slowing down. I press on the right rudder. Gently the right wing, nose, and left wing describe a beautiful arc and the aeroplane starts diving earthwards.

Impressed with my performance, seduced by my own ego, I leave my mind back there in that gorgeous balletic curve, and forget to do anything else.

The instructor wakes me up. 'Throttle off. Stick back. Put on some g. Throttle gently forward as the nose comes through the horizon, and climb away.'

'Sorry, sir. May I try again?'

I swear that this time I will keep my brain in one piece. Speed, climb, hold it just short of vertical, rudder, throttle off, over she goes. Ground straight ahead, centre rudders, look up, pull out with plenty of g. Power on, gently. Looking good.

'Watch the nose. Too high. You'll stall.'

Convinced that that was as near perfect as I am ever likely to make it, and fired by ludicrously excessive ambition, I decide that I want to try a stall turn to the left. My instructor is not about to stop me if I show a determination to make a fool of myself. But the Students' Study Guide did warn me about the difficulties of a stall turn to the left. The problem arises partially from gyroscopic forces, which are a governing factor in the life of the pilot flying a propeller-driven aeroplane, and partially from the airflow along the fuselage from the propeller, which can have a vicious effect on the authority of the rudder.

'Start feeding the rudder in early, and get the power off in good time,' a considerate instructor has advised, when I was discussing stall turns to the left in the mess the previous night.

So let's try it. The entry is even better than the last one, and I check the pitch up carefully before the wing comes over beyond the vertical. Look upwards at the nose. The aircraft is losing speed. Feed in left rudder. It is looking perfect. Now it doesn't want to go. Go, damn you! The wings are behaving strangely, and I correct with aileron movement on the stick. It refuses to go, however much rudder I kick on. What now? Before I have time to think the problem through the aeroplane is over on to its back and into a vertical dive. Power off. At least I remember that.

'Centre everything.' I feel the instructor snap the stick and rudder into the centre. 'Look up. Pull to the nearest horizon. Power on and climb away.' He is very sympathetic. 'We told you it was difficult. But at least you recovered correctly. Remember to centre all the controls if things start to go wrong.'

The last variant I plan to try in this sortie is the enchantingly named Noddy stall turn. There does not seem to be much point to it in operational terms, but it is in the syllabus, it does present some interesting control problems, and, once mastered, it does demonstrate that the student is beginning to achieve a relatively advanced level of flying skill. The manoeuvre starts just like a stall turn, but I need to begin to think early. So, power on, dive to build up speed, then smartly pull into the climb, and relax the pitch as I approach the vertical. As the speed begins to reduce, I need to turn the nose off to the right, say 15 or 20 degrees, with a touch of rudder. The speed continues to decay, so quickly relax the right rudder and apply left rudder. The nose nods across to 15 or 20 degrees to the left of the vertical. Satisfactory so far. The interesting problem is that the aeroplane also rolls, and the wings do not want to stay in place as I nod the nose across from side to side. I start chasing the wing movements with the stick, trying to make some sense of its gyrations, but before we have sorted that out the speed has gone. Fortunately the nose is off to the right, not to the left, and I can pull the nose across right through the vertical, and over into a complete stall turn, with the right wing, the nose, and the left wing slicing in turn straight and true through the horizon. At last I find myself pointing towards the brown fields 5,000 ft below. And this time I remember to recover: power off, centre rudder, centre stick, stick back, pull on the g, nose through the horizon, ease the throttle fully forwards, and climb out.

'Good. Now take us back to base.'

If you were ever tempted to imagine that your life as a pilot would consist mainly of throwing an aeroplane about the sky with uninhibited abandon, you will be rapidly disabused when you see the learning load associated with your training, especially with the business of navigating. Piloting aeroplanes is, if nothing else, a profession, and years of professional learning are called for, to provide a foundation of knowledge that will support your activities in the air. Only with that knowledge can the pilot fly the aeroplane and operate it effectively as a weapons system.

Flying military aircraft is a cerebral business as much as it is a physical one. Of course, you need confidence and courage and aggression to go to war; equally you need the co-ordination and mechanical aptitude to control a complex machine at high speed. But few people realise that a fighter pilot needs a substantial amount of raw intelligence, to understand the workings of the aircraft, to grasp and interpret the workings of the weather system, and above all to be able to navigate the aircraft. At high speed, at low level, perhaps in hostile environment, and while concentrating on reaching and destroying an objective, the pilot has to know where he is, and where he is going. That involves calculating, recalculating, checking, and calculating again, almost always mentally, because even at 250 ft and 90 knots, still less 100 ft and 500 knots, there is no place for extensive map-reading and scribbling calculations on your kneepad.

If you ever wondered why the selection process laid such emphasis on your aptitude for making rapid mental calculations under pressure, you will find out when you begin to study the art of air navigation. And you will begin to believe that whoever compared the human brain to a computer might have been thinking of a trainee fighter pilot on a navigation sortie. Navigation is a skill that is built up gradually. Most military navigation is carried out with the aid of a 1:250,000 scale map. Students start with a simple point-to-point exercise, performed with the help of the instructor. Then they expand that to a set triangular course, flown first under supervision and then solo. Finally they venture out on an exercise which they plan themselves and fly solo, all at medium level.

Eventually, since the Royal Air Force is a low-level air force, this experience has to be converted into the rather different world of the low-level navigator. It is different because features which from medium level bear some resemblance to their representation on the map, look very unlike them at low level. A diamond-shaped wood looks much like a diamond-shaped wood from 2,000 ft; from 250 ft it might look just like a line of trees. And a feature that is visible from three miles from medium level might well be hidden by the contours until you are overhead as you approach it at low level. There are other complications. At 250 ft you have to fly the aircraft with considerable care. Taking your eyes off the way ahead to search your map for a feature is not recommended. Holding the map up in front of you for a cursory glance is all the map-reading that you can afford to allow yourself. Navigating an aircraft is a painstaking process of assembling information, selecting and grading it, then amending it in action to arrive at the desired result. It starts slowly, then gathers pace until in the final stages the pressure can be unsupportable.

That is when the successful survive. As ever, the secret lies in the preparation.

Some of the navigation exercises are over a set course, and parts of the planning can be completed well in advance of the flight. Wise students give themselves ample time to study the course. Some preparation can be done only when the conditions on the day, notably the forecast wind, are ascertained in the hour or so before the flight.

The triangular course exercise runs as follows. First draw a pencil line on the map from the point where the exercise starts to the first turning point, or waypoint, then to the second, and on to the final point. Highlight the pencil lines in bright yellow for maximum visibility. Then redraw the lines over the yellow in black felt-tip or ball-point. Break the line at any usable feature, so that the feature remains visible, and is conspicuous by the gap in the line. Study the route for any features that should be visible from the air at the altitude you intend to fly. Choose features that lie between six and ten minutes' flying time apart, at your standard cruising speed, and circle them in black. Draw a dotted line back from each waypoint at an angle of 5 degrees on one side of each segment of the track. Now settle down and study the map until you know the area as if you had flown over it many times. Study especially the significant features. Identify the highest relevant obstacle, so that you can establish your safety altitude. A relevant obstacle is the highest point within 30 nautical miles (nm) of your planned route, either to the side or round the ends. Add a margin of 1,000 ft then round it up to the nearest 100 ft. If you find yourself in cloud at any stage, that is the height you fly to, before you do anything else to sort yourself out. If there are mountains around where you fly, increase the margin above the highest object to 5,000 ft.

You can do a little more preparatory work by drawing in your heading boxes and fuel circles. The flight operations room has a template for the job, and you simply draw round the inside of the shape, as on a stencil, and draw lines across the shapes. You can fill in the safety altitudes for each leg in red.

Just before the flight, you will obtain the meteorological forecasts, notably the predicted winds. Now comes the activity familiar to all civilian pilots, the computer calculation. The flight computer is a circular device with a sliding scale, on which a pilot can

calculate almost any information relevant to his flight, with reasonable accuracy. In civilian flying it is a plastic apparatus; the military
use a metal version. If you take into account the magnetic variation
along the route, you can work out your magnetic track. Then
enter the predicted wind on the face of the computer, and with a
couple of movements of the sliding scale and the circular heading
scale you can work out the heading you should fly to compensate
for the predicted wind. You can also calculate the groundspeed
you will achieve, again taking into account the strength and
direction of the wind, and its effect on your aircraft at your planned
airspeed.

Flip over the computer, and with a turn of the circular slide rule
you can calculate the fuel you are going to use for each leg, and
the time each leg will take, at the groundspeeds which you have
already calculated. How you actually work out these items is the
subject of a separate book entirely, but the average pilot can, with
the help of his instructor, quickly become adept at handling the
flight computer.

Now you can begin to fill in on the map the details which you
have calculated, and also fill in the log card, which is a second
vital catalogue of information. You have already drawn the outline
of a heading box for each leg. Enter into it the heading you should
fly, the flight level or altitude you intend to fly at, and the indicated
airspeed, all in black. You already have the safety altitude entered
in red. You have also already drawn the outlines of your fuel
circles, in suitable places so as not to obscure vital map features,
and you can work back from your final objective, stating in the
top half of the circle how much fuel you expect to have in your
tanks at that point, and in the bottom half the fuel you actually
need at that point in order to fly home. Now colour in red all the
relevant restricted and danger areas along your route, and write
their upper limits clearly inside the boundary. Colour all controlled
airspace in the region, in blue, and mark in the altimeter setting
regions, in green. Add any other relevant items in yellow. From
the ground-speed you have calculated, you need to enter the times
for each leg. At the beginning of each leg you draw a small symbol
to show that here you start the stop watch, with a similar symbol
at the end of the leg to show the time which the leg will take. And
you similarly mark the stop-watch time against each of the features
you have ringed. Then you divide each leg up into two-minute

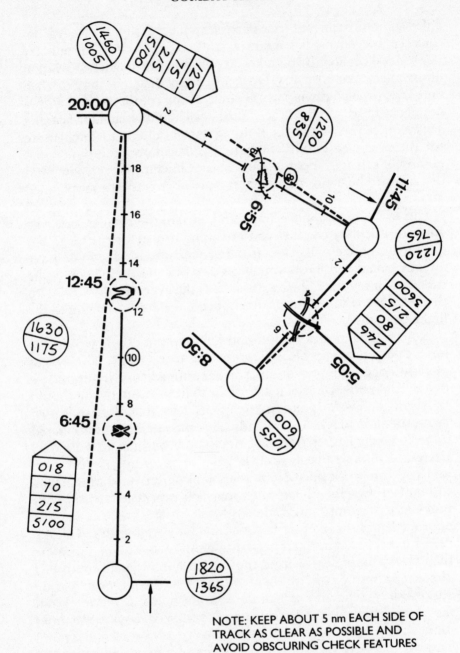

NOTE: KEEP ABOUT 5 nm EACH SIDE OF
TRACK AS CLEAR AS POSSIBLE AND
AVOID OBSCURING CHECK FEATURES

*Fig. 5* The map preparation completed for a three-leg sortie; headings, speeds, heights, times, fuel state, and easily recognisable features are included for each leg

intervals, and mark the leg clearly with a short cross line, and the elapsed time against it in black marker.

Two tasks remain. One is to enter almost all the information you have amassed into the flight log. The other is to fold your map so that you have a clear view of each leg. If you need to, you can cut off and throw away any unwanted area of map for the sake of convenience. The Royal Air Force does not mind the expense. Civilian pilots could not be so profligate. You now have in your hand a map which bears every relevant piece of information for the flight you intend to make, and from your study of the night before you are totally familiar with the area over which you intend to fly. Check the NOTAMS for any special instructions, and write in the direction and distance off track of a suitable diversion airfield.

You have a beautiful plan. Unfortunately, aviation being the inexact science that it is, you can be certain that the plan represents no more than your intention at the start of the exercise. The opportunities for it to go wrong in flight are legion. You have, for example, been able to calculate your heading and groundspeed only according to the meteorological forecast of the wind for the altitude you plan to fly. The wind is notoriously unpredictable and always variable, so it is unlikely to conform to the plan. You will almost certainly find yourself off track, and with your groundspeed failing to take you as far along the track as you anticipated that it would. You have no other choice but to resort to your training, your instinct, and your brain power, and adapt your plan to account for this unceasing fluidity.

There are, mercifully, techniques for replanning in flight, although achieving a usable command of them is a challenge. As you begin to learn some of these techniques, you might even begin to understand the relevance of the tests which you survived in the hangar long ago during your selection process, when an instinctive understanding of angles, levers, and the fundamentals of geometry came to your aid. The first and most important weapon in your mental navigation armoury is known as the 1-in-60 rule. It states simply (*see fig.* 6) that if you are one unit of measurement away from your intended course after 60 units of measurement, you will have experienced one degree of drift. So if you can establish that after 30 nm you are three miles away from where you should be on your course, you are on a 6-degree drift. Two nautical miles away after 40 nm, that is a 3-degree drift.

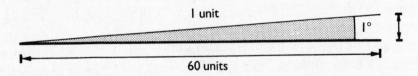

*Fig.* 6 The 1-in-60 rule, essential for revising your heading after diverging from track

The second useful accomplishment is one designed to take you as efficiently as possible towards your waypoint. It is known as the closing angle, or C A. First you need to establish your drift, which you can do either by using the 1-in-60 rule, or by reading it off your map by referring to the 5-degree lines that you drew on each sector. It is not difficult, if you have a 5-degree angle on one side of your track, to estimate with fair accuracy the angle by which you have drifted off track. The diagram illustrates the principle. If you have established your position off track, and estimated the angle of drift, you also need to estimate the proportion of the leg that you have flown. Then you can rapidly work out the closing angle to reach your way-point. For example: half-way along the leg, and 3 degrees to the left of track – turn 6 degrees right; 10 degrees off track to the right, and three-quarters of the leg flown – turn 40 degrees to the left.

Once completely understood and mastered, those two rules will get you safely to your intended destination.

Navigation now becomes interesting. Supposing that half-way along your final leg you learn that the airfield where you intended to land is closed. You have to find a diversion, and calculate the track you need to fly to get there, as well as your heading to achieve that track, and your estimated time of arrival. Map up. You have a diversion airfield marked. And there is a feature about five miles ahead on your present track that will give you a good clear turning point from which to divert.

You need to know first the distance from that point to the diversion airfield. You have all sorts of clues available that will help you to estimate the distance. Some students carry a pencil notched with a knife at intervals of 5 nm. The grid squares on your map are at 10-kilometre intervals, and you know that 10 km is 5.5 nm, as near as necessary. But the simplest is probably the end bone of your thumb, the exact length of which, in terms of the nautical miles it represents on the map, you have previously calculated.

You also have aids to help you estimate the bearing from diversion point to diversion airfield. You might carry a transparent plastic compass rose that you can stick on the face of the map. But at low level you will have little time for that, so you had better learn to estimate with the eye. You can use the grid lines on the map, and estimate angles between them. With growing experience, and a lot of diligent practice on the test chart on the navigation planning room wall, you should be able to arrive at an estimated angle accurate to within 2 or 3 degrees. With the distance, your track, and your airspeed known, you should be able to get there safely and calculate your estimated time of arrival — in still air.

But where is the wind? And what will it do to the plan? This is a new problem. Are you up to solving it? You are looking for the heading to fly, to achieve the track you have estimated. The wind will also effect your ground-speed, so you will have to recalculate that. Then you must calculate the time it will take you to fly the distance you have estimated at that groundspeed. How do you do all of that? By the following steps.

First, drift. Think about the wind. If it is less than 10 per cent of your true airspeed (TAS) you can ignore it. If it is greater than that you will have to compensate for the drift it imposes. The first task is to calculate the maximum drift you would encounter if the wind were effectively at 90 degrees to your track. By fairly simple mathematics it so happens that the drift is equal to the value of the windspeed divided by the true airspeed in miles per minute. If the wind is 20 knots, and your TAS is 120 knots, or 2 mpm, the maximum drift is 10 degrees. If you are flying at 240 knots, or 4 mpm, and the wind speed is 30 knots, the maximum drift is a quarter of 30, say 8 degrees. In fact, you picked up the predicted wind at the met briefing first thing that morning, so you can calculate the maximum drift before you set out. But the wind is rarely at 90 degrees, so we have to work out what proportion of the maximum drift it will impose on the aircraft, depending on the angle at which it is striking us.

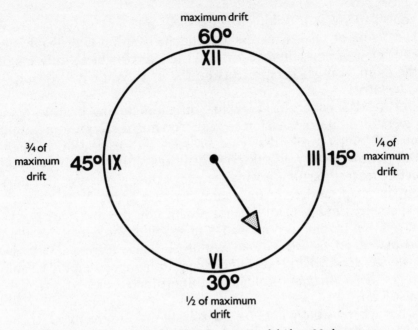

*Fig. 7* The clock code used for simple calculations of drift; a 20-degree wind angle would produce one-third of the maximum possible drift

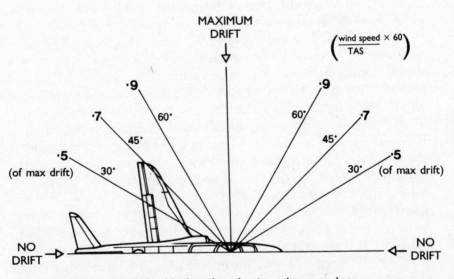

*Fig. 8* A more accurate drift table, based on the sine rule, to produce a proportion of the maximum possible drift

The answer lies in the sine rule. That (*see Fig. 7*) tells us that the magnitude of the drift will vary according to the sine of the angle between the track and the wind. You know what direction the wind is coming from: work out the angle relative to the direction of our track. Track 120, wind 180 degrees. Wind angle 60 degrees. Working out sine 60 in flight is impossible, without sine tables or a calculator, so you need a mentally usable method. A simple device is to think of a clock. Think of the angle in minutes, and convert the minutes into fractions of an hour. If the wind angle is 15 degrees, think of it as one-quarter of an hour, so regard that as a quarter of the maximum drift. In our second example we calculated that the maximum drift was 8 degrees, so the actual drift will be 2 degrees. If the wind angle is 30 degrees, that is half of the hour, so the actual drift will be half of the maximum drift. If the wind angle is 45 degrees, regard it as producing three-quarters of the maximum drift, or in our example 6 degrees. For 60 degrees or more, don't worry about it. Just use the whole of the maximum drift as the actual drift.

An alternative method is to use a drift table (*see Fig. 8*). If the wind angle is 30 degrees use half of the maximum drift. If it is 45 degrees use seven-tenths. If it is 60 degrees use nine-tenths. More – use it all.

Now what about the strength of the wind? How will that effect our flight in terms of ground-speed? If the wind were on the nose we could simply subtract windspeed from true airspeed to give our ground-speed, or add it for a tail wind. But the wind is rarely on the nose or the tail. So we have to add or subtract only a proportion of the windspeed. To calculate that proportion, we need to apply the cosine rule. All you have to do is apply the cosine of the wind angle. Deduct the wind angle from 90 degrees, and then work the magic of the clock face again. The component of head or tail wind you have to deduct or add to give your ground-speed is worked according to the proportions of the hour, as before. If the wind angle is 30 degrees, 90 minus the wind angle is 60 degrees. Sixty on the clock face is the whole of the component, so for a wind angle of 30 degrees you can add or subtract the whole of the windspeed. For a wind angle of 60 degrees, add 30 minutes' worth, or half of the wind component.

Now we know the heading to fly in order to compensate for drift, and the groundspeed we will achieve. How long will this leg take us? We have estimated the leg from diversion point to diversion airfield as 20 nm, and our groundspeed as 110 knots. You will recall the simple formula that tells you: time is equal to distance divided by speed. To arrive at the number of minutes for which you must fly, you need to divide the speed in knots by 60. Then to find the time you need to divide 20 by the result. Now in all seriousness, with a speed of 110 knots, that calculation is impossible.

Never mind, the fighter pilot has the solution at hand. The key lies in rounding up or down to the nearest usable figure, say 90, 120, 180, or 240 knots. 110 knots is pretty near to 120 knots, which is 2 mpm. At 2 mpm 20 miles will take 10 minutes. We are going to fly at 1/12th slower than that, which for these approximate purposes is about a tenth, so add a tenth to the time. We can expect to be overhead the diversion airfield in 11 minutes. Here is the diversion point, so turn on to the heading, start the watch, and put the map away to see what happens. That, at least, is the theory, and many a fighter pilot's potential career has foundered on whether he could grasp that theory and put it into practice in the air, under pressure, or not.

Let us find out. Let us go and fly one of the many check-flights that the fighter pilot must undergo in the course of his training. The watershed in the life of the aspiring fighter pilot on the EFTS is a notorious little event known as Trip 35, or Sortie 35, or Exercise 35. It is your first real check-ride. The thirty-fifty event in the flying training syllabus sounds like a simple affair, and many students have no difficulty with it. That does not alter the fact that it looms, like Beecher's Brook, as the great obstacle on the first lap of the course. Pass this one, the students tell themselves, and they can pass anything. The test is rather a flexible event, and the instructors try to play down its importance, not least to avoid overwhelming the students with fear. It is true, nevertheless, that if a student passes this test, he will probably pass the final test in the EFTS course, and if he passes that he will, statistically, be unlikely to fail at any future hurdle in the basic flying training area. Trip 35, inevitably, becomes a critical item in the selection process.

'Right, David. The time has come for your first major test in the course. I shall not ask you to demonstrate anything that you have not been taught or had time to practise. At some point in the test I shall ask you to demonstrate an emergency, either forced landing without power, or engine failure on take-off, or both. I would like you to carry out touch drills to show what you would do. You will have the opportunity to show me any flying that you want to, but I shall certainly ask you to demonstrate the stall and recovery from the stall, spin and recovery, incipient spin and the recovery procedure. I shall ask you to demonstrate medium turns and steep turns, and the basic aerobatics that you have learned, including the loop, the barrel roll, and the stall turn.'

The test flight lasts about an hour. Some students are petrified by this make-or-break sortie. One young woman student at the London University Air Squadron put tests in their proper perspective: 'I look on them as just another flight; forget about the test side of it and enjoy it.' But when your career depends on it, it is difficult for most people to be quite so philosophical. The secret must be to prepare yourself as thoroughly as you can, then relax.

I should by now know my checks, so I need to make sure that my kit is in good order, stride confidently out to the aeroplane on the apron, walk around it to carry out the ground checks, helmet and parachute on, climb in, strap in, and work steadily and systematically through the cockpit checks. Forget nothing. Hands held aloft while the handler fits the starter cartridges, pull the starter ring, throttle to 1,200 rpm, continue the checks. It is my aeroplane. I have control. Cross hands to indicate checks complete, call the tower for permission to taxi, note and repeat back the airfield pressure and the active runway, and set off for the holding point. Five minutes of the test are completed, without disaster, and the aeroplane seems to be responding sensibly to inputs from my feet. Turn into wind for the power checks, continue to the holding point, and report, 'Sierra Zero Four ready for take-off.'

There is a delay while two aircraft, one on finals and one downwind, complete their circuits and land. Delays are useful pointers. Can I keep calm and use the time to think over what I intend to do, and run through the actions and checks? Or do the empty minutes begin to rattle me and make me nervous? I have got this far without being pulled up by the examiner, so I probably have all the checks right. Keep the rpm on the requisite 1,200, and stay calm. I rest my gloved hands in my lap. Now it is my turn.

On to the runway. Line up. Check the runway against the DI and make sure that it is clear of obstructions. Parking brake off. Full power, steer with the feet, and don't worry about the

Chipmunk's swerve. As the rudder takes full effect the aeroplane straightens out. Stick forward to lift the tailwheel. The speed is 60 knots, so stick back to rotate. At 200 ft flaps up, check brakes, check temperatures and pressures, look out. Keep looking out. If I see and report other traffic before the examiner sees it, it will do my prospects no harm.

At 500 ft I turn on to the heading to take me out into the local area. What have I forgotten? Nothing I can think of. So keep the wings level and keep climbing. Relax and fly. The departure checks! Report to the tower. Change the altimeter to the QNH setting for the local area. Fuel pump off. I wish I had learned the checks more fully, but perhaps I completed them just in time to stop him thinking I had forgotten them. What next?

'Would you like to see the stall first, sir?' Good idea to take the initiative. He agrees. Through the transition level, so change the altimeter to 1,013, and calculate the safe stalling height. Transition height plus 300 ft for ground level plus recovery height needed of 500 ft is 4,100 ft. Round that up to 4,500 ft for safety.

Repeat the checks aloud, and in detail. HASEL L is the easy one to remember. Then straight into the stall with power off, stick back to hold up the nose and maintain height, and you can just feel the burbling of the airflow as it begins to break away from the wing. That is known as the light buffet, like pebbles being dropped. Watch the height and speed. And the airflow begins really to break away, like stones being thrown – the heavy buffet. 'Recovering now, sir.' Throttle forward, and stick forward centrally. If the aircraft starts to yaw to the side correct it with rudder. Now stick back and with full power climb away. 'Height loss about 200 ft, sir. Would you like to see one with full flap, sir?'

'Yes please.' Back up to 4,500 ft and carry out the abbreviated HELL checks. Height, engine, location and lookout turns. With full flap on, straight into the stall, and it happens much more quickly, so, 'Recovering now, sir,' and stick forward, a touch of power, stick back and full power and climb away.

'Thank you, flaps up then, and I'm pulling the throttle. You have an engine failure. What are you going to do?'

What I actually do is struggle to keep some semblance of order in my brain so that I can fight off the panic and remember the sequence.

First thing: lower the nose to get a safe gliding speed, say 70

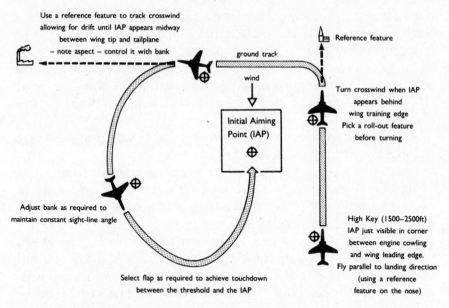

Use a reference feature to track crosswind
allowing for drift until IAP appears midway
between wing tip and tailplane
– note aspect – control it with bank

ground track

Reference feature

wind

Turn crosswind when IAP
appears behind
wing training edge
Pick a roll-out feature
before turning

Initial Aiming
Point (IAP)

Adjust bank as required to
maintain constant sight-line angle

High Key (1500–2500ft)
IAP just visible in corner
between engine cowling
and wing leading edge.
Fly parallel to landing direction
(using a reference
feature on the nose)

Select flap as required to achieve touchdown
between the threshold and the IAP

*Fig.* 9 The pattern for the simulated emergency 'forced landing without
power', from high key to initial aiming point

knots. Now look for a suitable place to land. There's the wind
from left to right so I shall try to land from right to left as I look
at it. 'I'm going to land in that big field just ahead of the left wing
with the sheep in it and the trees in the corner.'

Now the checks, out loud: 'Fuel. Check tanks, primer locked,
fuel pump on. Engine instruments. Carburettor heat. Magnetos
both on. No clues there, so we will have to complete the landing.'

'Power on to clear the engine.' Hold the nose down as we do
that to maintain the flight path. Lucky we remembered that one.

Look for the high key position of 1,500 ft, going in the direction
of landing. Still some height to lose so call the emergency: *Mayday
Mayday Mayday. Sierra Zero Four. Engine failure forced landing
one mile north of . . . Mayday Mayday.* Power on to clear the
engine. The ground is beginning to take shape now. Check height.
It is close to the high key position. Luckily the field is still in
sight and I am heading north-west which is my planned landing
direction. Prepare for the landing. 1,500 ft so keep turning now.
Straps tight. Fuel cock off. Fuel pump off. Magnetos off. Master
switch off. 1,000 ft and still going round. Turn now. Flaps to
intermediate, not bad. 800 ft and it looks as if we might make it.

No obstructions in the field. 'I'm going to select full flap now, sir, and we should land in the first third of the field.' 600 ft, and dropping like a stone. 500 ft and the contours are beginning to come up round the ears. 'Going around now, sir.' Full power and nose up and climbing, so one stage of flap in, and hold the speed at 70 knots with the stick, then second stage of flap in, and climbing steadily.

'I'd like you to take us back up to a suitable height now so that you can show me your aerobatics.'

Exhausted already, I wrestle with the problems not so much of flying but of memory. What have I left out? What do I need to do? Can I hold my performance together through more of this? Can I remember the aerobatics? And in the right sequence? Don't rush it. Calculate the height again and think out the checks. In fact, it would be worth some checks now. Let him know I am doing them. Fuel, engine temperatures and pressures within limits. Say them out loud. Now we are at 4,500 ft. HASELL checks again. Height: adequate for the exercise. Airframe. Security. Engine. Location. Lookout. Take your time. Don't rush them, but don't dawdle.

'I'd like to do a loop first, followed by a barrel roll, then a stall turn, sir.'

'Go ahead then, when you are ready.'

Throttle fully forward and nose down. 110 knots. Look up above the canopy. 120 knots. Pull back on the stick. Remember to use my feet to counter the torque from the propeller. Relax the back pressure at the top of the loop. Watch for the ground, now pull some g as we go down the other side. Level out. Check the height. Check full power. Nose down again. 110 knots. Roll to the right. 120 knots, now pitch up and try to remember what I worked out about the barrel loop. Pitch right up, nose well above the horizon. Apply aileron left, hold the pitch, hold the aileron, hope for the best. Relax the pitch as we go inverted, relax the roll, and a bit more pitch to pull us level. Check the direction. And another barrel roll to the right. First lower the nose to increase the speed. Then dive left, then pull up. Now roll right, through the inverted. Relax the pitch. Hold the roll. Coming the right way up. And relax the roll, centre the stick, and pull back a little to bring us level.

What did I promise next? Ah, the stall turn, to the right for the sake of simplicity. Nose down to 110 knots, remember to look up. Remember to use my feet. Pull up quite briskly. Fly the aeroplane. I seem to be doing all right. Relax the back pressure before it goes over the vertical. Hold it like that. Look along the wing. Look ahead, we have almost stopped climbing. I should monitor the instruments but I daren't stop to look at them. Apply right rudder. The starboard wing drops obediently, and the nose follows it over. Hold it. Going down now. So power off. Centre rudder. Pull some g. Look up. Stop staring over the nose. As the nose comes through the horizon apply full power. No, less severe on the throttle. And I am climbing again. Did I get away with it?

'I'd like to see a spin now, please.'

Hell, I'd forgotten about the spin. Start climbing. Start calculating the minimum height for the spin. Do it out loud. Write it down on the kneepad, if I can get the pencil out of my flying suit pocket. Transition level plus 300 ft for the ground. Plus 3,000 ft to abandon the aeroplane. The aeroplane! Remember to fly the aeroplane. Add 1,200 ft for four turns of a spin. 8,500 ft altogether. 'I'm rounding up to 9,000 ft, sir, if that is all right.'

The aeroplane grinds interminably upwards. You wonder if we are still in the local area. Well, time to go for it. More HASELL checks, including the fuel state. And make sure we have a clear sight of the ground, though it looks murky on this winter's afternoon. Those poor people down there are in shadow from the distant cloud. Stop dreaming. 'Spinning to the left, sir.' Throttle off, hold the stick back, right back, and full left rudder. *Wham*. Over she rolls, and into the spin. Check the turn needle. It is over to the left. Count the turns. One, two, three, that's enough. 'Recovering Now, sir.' Throttle off, spinning left, so full right rudder, stick firmly forwards, spin stops. Centre rudder, pull out of the dive, firmly, with some g. Nose coming up, throttle forwards to full power. '1,200 ft height lost, sir.'

'If you would like to take us back towards the airfield, please.'

A gentle descending turn down to 2,000 ft in this area should do then we'll fly back. But in what direction? I try to calculate on the way down. We came out on 270 degrees, so 90 degrees should start us home. Give or take the wind from the north-east. And what do I need to do next? First the cruise checks, then the approach checks. Level out at 2,000 ft and set the power to 2,300 rpm to give us 90 knots.

'If you would just show me a medium turn through 360 degrees here, please.'

Look out, then roll on the bank, and turn at about 30 degrees. Hold the nose on the horizon. Look out of the cockpit. Don't pull too hard on the stick. Roll out on 90 degrees again. Fly straight and level.

'And a steep turn, please, to the right, and roll out on a heading of Zero Three Zero.'

'I'd like to carry out the cruise checks first, please.' I refuse to let myself be hurried. Fuel, engine instruments, directional gyro against compass. The direction indicator is out by 30 degrees for a start. It is a good job I checked it. Radio and altimeter. Altimeter! I forgot to reset the altimeter as we came down through the transition level. Set it to the regional QNH. What was it? Why not ask for it?

'Sierra Zero Four, request regional QNH?' Air traffic provides it. I acknowledge. 'Sierra Zero Four,' and set it, and apologise. 'Sorry, sir, I should have set that earlier.' I have to climb back up to 2,000 ft, to compensate for the mistaken height. 'Steep turn to the right on to Zero Three Zero, sir.' Roll on the bank, a bit of throttle, hold up the nose. Look out at the wing, and at the horizon. That seems to be going well. And check the direction indicator: 030 coming up, so roll out early, throttle back at the same time, and reset the throttle.

'Now, if you would like to call the airfield, make the approach and join the circuit for a standard approach and roller.'

What next? First find the airfield. There are the four power stations, and the river. Yes, it is all becoming familiar. And the town down there, so it should be . . . yes there it is. Now call the tower, repeat back the runway and altimeter QFE setting, for the airfield. Reset the altimeter. Now climb to 2,000 ft for the approach, and keep a very good lookout for circuit traffic. Cross over the threshold end of the runway, and out on to the dead side. Report dead side. Let down to 800 ft, turn and cross the upwind end of the runway. Hold the speed to 90 knots and the height exactly at 800 ft. Turn downwind. Carry out the downwind checks in good time, and report downwind: 'Sierra Zero Four downwind to roll.' Keep the wings level. Check the ball for balance. I keep forgetting that. The wind is blowing us away so turn towards the runway slightly. Pick the 400-ft point and when I come level with it start my finals turn. Throttle back to 70 knots, wait till the speed reduces and set the flaps to intermediate. Half-way round the turn look for 600 ft. Call finals. Set full flap. Fly through the doughnut. Over the 400-ft point, and everything is looking good. Point the nose at the threshold. Keep the speed accurate with the throttle. Play them gently, stick and throttle. Now over the threshold fly the aeroplane right down to the runway, and flare now. Hold the stick right back, and down she goes. Power on now, a touch of rudder, stick forward to lift the tailwheel, and 65 knots pull the stick back and off she lifts. Flaps to intermediate. After-take-off checks, turn now, flaps up.

'If you would make this a flapless landing please. Full stop.'

Everything seems to be all right so far. Level off at 800 ft. Call downwind, and my intention to make a full stop. Acknowledge ATC's response. Downwind checks. Track in for wind. Extend the downwind leg slightly for a shallow flapless approach. Pick the 400-ft point further out. Slow to 70 knots. Call finals. Get lined up. Nose slightly high. Fly right down. And hardly any flare. Throttle off, land, touch of rudder, stick right back, and a touch of brake before we turn off the runway and stop for the after-landing checks. Taxi in, and close down. Hands above the head for the ground crew. And out we climb. It has been a long sortie.

There is no indication from the examiner. He is quite matter-of-fact. 'Parachute and helmet to Safety Equipment, get yourself a cup of coffee, and meet me in the debriefing room in five minutes.'

I get there well before he does.

'Let's discuss how that went. First, you were a bit slow with your checks during the Forced Landing Without Power . . . '

I thought I had done quite well, but he is tearing my performance apart. There are comments about my aerobatics, height keeping, lookout, insufficient checks during straight and level flight.

'But your main fault is not using rudder enough to keep the ball in the centre to maintain balanced flight, especially during your aerobatics. And I want you to feel much freer with the aeroplane. At the moment you seem to be flying it by numbers, as if you are slightly frightened of doing something wrong. If you really flew the aeroplane the way you wanted to, you would get much more out of it. But, overall, you did quite well, and passed your Exercise 35.'

This examiner is one who will not tell a student he has passed until he has gone right through the debrief. He explains why: 'If I tell a student straight away that he has passed, his jaw will drop, he will be delighted with the news, and he will learn nothing more from that lesson.'

Back in the students' crew room, the atmosphere is becoming tense. Three students from this flight have failed the exercise. Those who fail have two more hours of instruction, with a new instructor, who might well be the examiner who failed them, followed by a second test, which is their last chance. One has failed completely and been offered a degree course and a new career in the engineering branch. He is contemplating whether his love of the service is strong enough to overcome his disappointment at not making the grade as aircrew. Another, on his second test, applied too much rudder at the top of a barrel roll and ended up with an inadvertent autorotation, from which his instructor had to recover. That was the end of his chances. Another got right through the test then showed that he could not fly straight and level in the circuit. The ones who have failed have formed into a small clique, gathering together in good-humoured sympathy. It is embarrassing for those who have passed; 28 per cent of all the students who embark on this course fail to make it, most of them at the Trip 35 stage. On some courses the entire flight sails through the course and all pass the tests without difficulty. That means that on some other courses, most of the students must fail.

The only consolation is that the standard of instruction, and the evenness of the testing procedure, is checked ruthlessly and frequently by the 'standards' personnel from the Central Flying School. And the instructors go through systematic crew training to ensure that they are doing their jobs properly, and examining students to the same levels. Failing students is a process carried out with honesty and straightforwardness. It is designed to protect the failures from danger to themselves, as much as to protect the air force from the failures.

What are they looking for in a good student, and how do they know when they have one? According to Sq Ldr Denis Winterbottom, flight commander at EFTS: 'The first characteristic we look for is a natural sympathy with mechanical objects. Even when a student is first taxiing the aircraft you can see a natural aptitude. Some students are inclined to lower the nose when you tell them to raise it. Some get over that. A very good guide is their natural reaction to what is happening around them. If the student is comfortable, and responds without hesitation, it shows he is going in the right direction. A really good student seems to know what you want him to do even before you have finished showing him. He gives you a feeling of being with you, not behind you. He will be looking around, relaxed, and knowing where he is. He will know where base is, and have a feel for the position he is in and the direction he needs to go to fly home. Fewer than a quarter of students are like that.

'A good student is a natural in the air. He has lots of motivation. Motivation is very important. If he has the dedication, he stands a good chance of success.'

# 6

## Streaming

There is a third way into a fast-jet flying career with the Royal Air Force, which misses out both the pitfalls of the EFTS Chipmunk course, and the enjoyable club world of the university air squadrons. Some people move into military flying along this route straight from school. Others join following abortive starts in other careers. In either case, these are recruits who already have in their log-books 30 or more hours of authorised flying tuition.

They might be keen enthusiasts who have gone out and taken flying lessons at their own expense, and probably will be equipped with the unprepossessing little brown document that the British Civil Aviation Authority issues as a Private Pilot's Licence. Alternatively they might have been recipients of a Royal Air Force flying scholarship. In one of the more notable examples of self-interested generosity exhibited by the British taxpayer, the Royal Air Force offers flying scholarships to numbers of young men (and now women) in the 16–18 age group. The scholarship provides 30 hours of free flying at a flying club near to the student's home. Thirty hours is not enough for a PPL, but any holder who does not manage to raise the extra money to complete the necessary hours is not showing the kind of initiative that will get him into the ranks of fast-jet pilots in the Royal Air Force.

Provided the student has at least 30 hours of flying training on a recognised course, he skips the EFTS Chipmunk course, and goes straight to Basic Flying School. That means the Tucano. If he has no previous military flying experience, the Basic Flying School course lasts for 70 hours. If he arrives from the EFTS or a UAS, the course lasts for 50 hours. The difference is in the early stages, and mid-way through the two courses merge and everybody is doing the same flying.

The Tucano, to the pilot coming new to it from those few hours at a private flying club, is a formidable handful of aircraft. It has two novel attributes. First, it is a tandem-seat aircraft, in which the student sits in the front seat with the instructor behind him in a separate cockpit. The same applies to the UAS student, who has previously flown only the side-by-side Bulldog. In the Tucano aircraft there will be none of that intimidating and often disconcerting presence lurking in the corner of the eye. The tandem seat has some advantages. It means that the student does not have to learn two sets of references, for example the picture out of the cockpit in a right-hand circuit and the different picture for a left-hand circuit. It also gives him a highly developed sense of responsibility for the aircraft, as he tends not to expect the instructor to be instantly available to correct his mistakes. And it give him an early feel for the kind of aircraft he will be flying next if he is selected for combat training. It also has disadvantages, in that the instructor cannot see directly whether the student is handling the controls correctly. He can see only the effects of any mishandling. Overall, students and instructors alike seem to favour the tandem-seat arrangement.

Secondly, the student will, of course, not have had the experience of strapping into an ejection seat before.

You have gone through ground school, and been through a strict simulator preparation, but nothing has quite been able to prepare you for single-seat flying in an aircraft with so much power available. You are strapped in. You feel alone. Somewhere behind you your instructor is strapping himself into the rear cockpit. You are on your familiarisation flight, your first acquaintance with the Tucano. Below you the ground seems yards away. You begin to realise that you are in an aircraft that is as dramatically different from any private aircraft you have ever flown as it is from the modestly powered military primary training aircraft. As you taxi out from the apron, the difference begins to become startling. The Tucano is a thoroughbred. The study guide urges you not to exceed a brisk walking pace in turns or in congested areas. It allows you to taxi 'briskly' on long straight sections and in good conditions. The Tucano needs no telling. Where you have before ridden only docile steeds, you are now on one that positively gallops along the taxiway. If you had ever driven a high-powered sports car, you will recall how it made your family saloon seem tame. This aircraft is an order again in advance of that. You feel the responsiveness with your first taxiing manoeuvre in this aircraft. Press the rudder to operate the nosewheel steering. Touch the brake if you need a sharper turn, and the aircraft obeys, and romps eagerly towards the threshold. There, once cleared on to the runway, line up and complete the checks. You have learned them painstakingly, and practised them in the simulator, and you have completed the pre-take-off checks.

'Tango One request take-off.'

In front of you the propeller is working away with irresistible urgency. Hold the aircraft on the toe-brakes. Advance the throttle to 50 per cent power. The aircraft is desperate to go. Check the rpm, exhaust gas temperature, and oil pressure and temperature. Release the brakes and apply full power. Get the feel of the rudders with your toes, and hold the aircraft straight as it begins to sprint down the centreline. A touch more right rudder to keep it straight. Check the temperature and torque. Keep an eye on the speed. It reaches 75 knots. Ease the stick back, and the aircraft lifts off and begins to fly with glorious gathering speed, and an eagerness that no aircraft you have yet flown offers to you. It is a feeling that never leaves the pilot – the exhilarating sense of freedom every time your aircraft leaves the runway.

You are on your first circuit in this new aircraft, and the circuit develops with startling speed. Events follow one another in a bewildering rapid sequence. Gear up as soon as you are safely airborne. Feel for the lever; there is no time to look for it, but it is down there to your left. Flaps up; the lever is further back on your left side, and you have to ease it through a 'gate'. Put your left hand on the throttle again, and ease it back to give 60 per cent power. Adjusting the power requires no more than gentle pressure, and if you keep an eye on the torque meter, you can set it with extreme accuracy. But the faster the aircraft, the faster the circuit, and the busier, and more demanding, and more terrifying in these early stages.

Keep your eye on the height. At 500 ft, if you have climbed at about the right angle, you will be flying at 140 knots. Apply stick pressure to give you 45 degrees angle of bank. Keep an eye on the attitude indicator. It is your key instrument, so use it to check that you are not over-banked, but you should be able to judge 45 degrees by eye at this stage in your flying. Keep the aircraft coming round and climbing. At 900 ft you are approaching the circuit height of 1,000 ft, so ease the stick forward to level out. You will also need to pull the throttle back to reduce the power to 25 per cent, or you will speed up in level flight, and the whole circuit will go wrong.

Your hands are working independently, but not badly. You have practised in the simulator, but now the whole circuit depends on your skill and presence of mind. You have memorised, and rehearsed over and over again in your mind, the key points in the circuit. Some people say that it amounts to flying by numbers, and flying by numbers is frowned on by those who value airmanship above all else. But you might as well know the numbers anyway, and get them right, and then you can show off your flying skills without making mistakes.

Now we are at 1,000 ft, and 140 knots, and 25 per cent torque, and we can level the wings and fly parallel with the runway for a few seconds. Make the downwind call. The lesson plan is to practise circuits continuously, so: 'Tango Three downwind. Roll.' Stay parallel with the runway, and work to maintain the right height. Think about the wind. There is always a crosswind component in the circuit. Flying would be easier without any wind, but at 1,000 ft there is always a wind, so you had better learn to take it into account. Where is it? And how strong? There is a calculation to do to work out the drift exactly, but at this stage there is no time. The wind was from the right on take-off, so in this right-hand circuit it will be making us drift in towards the runway. Bank to ease the nose to the left a few degrees, then level out.

Make the downwind checks.

Watch for the end of the runway. There it is already, out on the wing. Now estimate the spot where you will roll out on short finals. Look diagonally across 55 degrees ahead of you and towards the runway. In your mind visualise the point where that line intersects the runway centreline. That will be the roll-out point, where we level the wings and fly to the threshold. But here we can usefully cheat, or more correctly use local terrain to legitimate advantage. On this approach there is a convenient farmhouse. When that is off the end of the wing, tip in for finals. Ease off the power to 20 per cent torque. Select flaps down. Call finals and your intentions: 'Tango Three finals, gear down. Roll.'

'Tango Three clear to roll.'

Acknowledge: 'Tango Three.'

Here you encounter again the old problem of controlling the aircraft in the final approach. In the first part of finals, the book advises you to use power to control the rate of descent, and adjust the attitude to control the speed. Nose up to slow down, nose down to speed up. Keep the turn going. Follow that ribbon of air. Remember the farmhouse. Half-way round the turn you should be at 650 ft. Watch the height. If you are not low enough, extend the turn by a margin. There is the farmhouse, and the runway beyond it. Roll out of the turn, and you should be lined up with the runway. Keep the descent going. Now on short finals you can simplify the technique. Just point the nose at the threshold and control the speed with the throttle. It should require only the most marginal adjustments, so it is a legitimate technique. Keep the speed right. That is vital.

Now the threshold is approaching, fast.

This really is the moment of truth. You realise suddenly that there is an instructor in the back seat. In the intensity of your concentration you had forgotten about him. He has not said a word for minutes. You ask yourself if that is a good sign or a bad sign. Meanwhile you have forgotten the wind. It has blown you beyond the centreline, and you have to struggle to get back in line with the runway. That means yawing the nose to the right, and suddenly you are flying on the wrong line, and at the wrong angle. The wind is blustery, and all your hopes for a smooth and straightforward approach begin to go awry. Try to keep the Tucano coming down, and before you can get the aircraft truly and accurately lined up, you are at the threshold. Stick pressure to hold up the nose, kick the aircraft straight, and hold it. It starts to climb again. Pull back the throttle to reduce the power, and ease the stick forward to lower the nose again. The aircraft lands, with a fearful bump, some way past the threshold. But at least you are down.

It has not been your best approach, by a long way, but you have made the landing, and there is nothing more you can do about that one, so concentrate on the rolling take-off. Hold back the stick, right into your stomach, to keep the nosewheel off the runway, and push the throttle steadily forward with your left hand to full power. The aircraft wants to yaw, so work your right foot to keep it straight. It is immensely, ludicrously, illogical – one hand back, the other hand forward, and your feet off the floor and pressing on the right side to turn to the right. But if you cannot handle those simple actions, however disconnected they might seem, you will not make a pilot of any sort, least of all a fast-jet pilot. After a moment of wavering, the aircraft straightens miraculously, more or less on the centreline, and you feel the punch of power in the small of your back. Think about the next move in the circuit. Before you know it, the aircraft is storming along at take-off speed and is lifting off, flying again, and under the control of that magic wand between your knees.

You have a new circuit to fly. Ditch the shame of that appalling earlier effort from your mind, and try to get this one right. Look for accuracy, and you will impress. Gear up. Flaps up. Pull the power back to 60 per cent, and look for 500 ft. Your eyes are everywhere. Hands everywhere. And this wickedly powerful aircraft is under your control. Enjoy it. Master it. Do that and you can become a pilot. You are certain of it. The next circuit develops, faster and more pressure-filled than anything you have ever flown before. You need to organise your thinking, to cope with the piling up of developments in front of you. It is that ability to cope with the rapid accumulation of events, and then to stay ahead of them, which will eventually determine your future as a pilot, or as something other than a pilot.

In the long run, the difference between the fast-jet world and other forms of flying, or not being allowed to fly at all, will depend on how well you can impress on your instructors and assessors your ability to cope with the unexpected in the course of a sortie; on how well you can organise your reactions and responses in sequence during a period of intense workload; and on how effectively you handle the aircraft in the air when the problems are beginning to stack up. Master the circuit, and you are on your way.

The basic flying training course – 70 hours of flying for the inexperienced, 50 for the experienced – describes exactly what it sets out to be: basic. Whatever your previous flying experience, the BFTS will start you again at the beginning, and will take you to the point where you are a fully competent pilot, versed in, if not yet master of, the simple skills of flying. You will be a pilot.

In the early stages of the course the basics facts of flying are covered again. Effects of controls, primary and secondary; straight and level; climbing and descending; basic turns; stalling, both clean and with the flaps and gear down in the approach configuration. By that time, when you have gone through ten lessons, you are ready to fly the circuit, and after that to go solo.

The elements in the syllabus are familiar to the student pilot, military and civilian, the world over. Once you can fly the aircraft, you will need to fly it outside the circuit, and for that you will need to learn to perform a forced landing. Then advanced turns, spinning and aerobatics.

By this stage, your flying experience will be departing from the familiar. Not only will you be flying in a distinctly military environment, with all that that entails, but will be covering subjects not familiar to you. If you have come from the private flying world you will probably never have experienced a full spin, and you will almost certainly have no experience of aerobatics.

If you have come through one of the military systems, you will still not have tried instrument flying, or low flying, or formation flying. In this course you will cover six disciplines of flying: visual, instruments, low flying, navigation, aerobatics, and night flying. Each is a new challenge, each an opportunity to succeed or fail.

And at the end of the course, if you survive, you will have the equivalent of a PPL together with an instrument rating and a night rating. In addition you will have aerobatics skills and low-flying skills which the private pilot will never encounter.

The Royal Air Force has begun to take steps to review and modernise techniques in several areas. The most notable of them is probably navigation. Students on the Basic Flying Course learn – or re-learn – the skills of both visual and radio navigation. To their credit, the architects of the course have simplified the visual navigation element in the training to its most basic. You learn navigation first at medium level, then at low level.

Before you are ever introduced to the radio aids which will help you chart your course, you need to learn, or in some cases re-learn, how to prepare and read a map. 240 knots is the basic flying speed in the Tucano. At that speed you will be covering four miles every minute, or a mile every 15 seconds. There is no time to make and correct errors.

As the course book points out, the secret is in the planning. As in other early elements of the course, the student in his first forays into navigation will be flying well-trailed courses, and during these early stages will be told the route the evening before. It leaves time for some preparation, although not for all of it. However, once you have drawn your track on the map, you can at least take it to a remote corner in the quiet of the evening and study the territory. The route itself will probably be unfamiliar, and most probably entirely new. It makes sense to approach it by studying the geographic features in detail, to build a picture of what you expect to see. It pays to draw a circle round the significant features to remind you to look for them in the course of the flight – that wood there; the church just off track at about half-way; that village; and the reservoir. But be careful, because in this part of rural England there are several reservoirs and you can easily locate the wrong one.

On the day of the flight you can complete the preparation by 'winding' the map. Find out from met the likely wind at your planned height. Then out with the Dalton map computer, calculate the drift, calculate the magnetic heading to steer for your track, and calculate the predicted airspeed. Mark the magnetic heading beside the track in its small box with the arrowhead. Mark off along the track the significant minute or half-minute marks which are close to clear features, for the speed you have calculated. You should be able to fly accurately round the course now, and arrive at each of the waypoints on track and on time.

So let's fly the route.

With your map ready, and the aircraft checked out, you need one simple instrument now on which you will rely implicitly. It is the stop-watch. The wise student remembers not to leave his in the aircraft; they are sought-after souvenirs. It is also said that the Royal Air Force is the only organisation that gives you a watch when you join and takes it away when you retire. Wind it up, slot it into its fixture, and set it going. Now stop it and press the reset button. You can be sure now that it is working.

From this point on your first full navigation exercise should be a routine series of events. Indeed, the new navigation is known as the 'event technique'. It runs as follows. Take off and fly to the starting point. Approach the starting point on the heading required for the first leg, with the bug set on the direction indicator. As you overfly the starting point, start the watch. Carry out your post-HAT checks (height, altitude, time) and note the next event.

It is at five minutes into the flight, and is a 'fix'. Put down the map, fly the heading, and look out. Keep an eye on the time, and after four minutes, pick up the map. Take care to fly the aircraft accurately and safely, and check the fix that should come up in one minute. It is the corner of the wood with the church spire to the right. There it is, at five minutes. Make any corrections in the course and speed, and note the next event, in this case the turning point at eight minutes. Put the map down, carry out the cruise checks, and look out. Fly the aircraft as accurately as you can.

A minute before your next event, pick up the map. Watch the clock, look out for the village with the church, and 'bug' the heading for the next leg. Carry out the pre-HAT checks. Eight minutes coming up, and the turning point looks correct, so turn on to the new heading. Note the next event. It is a fuel check at 10 minutes. Put the map down. Look out, and fly the aeroplane.

Maintaining your track and staying in full control of where you are above the features on the ground are only a part of the art of navigation. Even at this basic level of flying training, you are expected to keep to time. The allowable margin of error at a fix is plus or minus five seconds. It is not much. As you fly overhead the fix feature, check the time. While you are adjusting your track to compensate for the effect of the wind on that particular leg, adjust your speed also, by one knot for every second you are early or late. It takes the usual astute calculating ability. Hold that new speed accurately for four minutes, or until the next fix, where you can carry out an updated check. Now work out what the wind was actually doing to your aeroplane, in terms of track and speed, and estimate the real wind velocity, instead of working on the anticipated wind velocity. Calculate the new track and airspeed to compensate for your actual wind. You will not be able to hold this for long, because you will arrive shortly at your waypoint, and turn on to a new track altogether.

Pick up the map a minute before the turning point, and read off the new heading. Bug it. Look ahead for the turning point, check your height, altitude, airspeed, and time, but leave the stop-watch running. Now you are overhead the turning point, so roll into a 60-degree turn. If you have prepared the map correctly you will overfly a feature where you planned to roll out on the new heading. Roll to wings level on the new track, and carry out the post-HAT check (height, altitude, airspeed, and time). As soon as you are satisfied that you are established on the new track, note the time at the next fix, put the map down, and fly the aircraft. And look out.

The entire three-legged sortie continues like that, with the next event coming up on time. The mistake is to try to read your map all the time. And the secret of being able to avoid doing so is confidence – confidence that you have prepared your map accurately, that you are flying as you intended (it is surprising how many students set off on the reciprocal of their intended course) and confidence that if you fly the aircraft as you have been taught, you will arrive unerringly at the navigational fixes.

In practice, it rarely works out like that, and any route is full of problems which you must deal with or avoid. The event technique is designed to give you plenty of opportunity to fly the aircraft without looking down at the map. The time is best spent looking out for other aircraft, and in busy airspace such as that of the UK there are always other aircraft about. You also need to leave yourself time to deal with weather. The pilot's view of bad weather is different from that of the man on the ground. On the kind of day when you are likely to be flying at all, rain comes down in fairly localised 'cylinders' which the man on the ground experiences as showers. You cannot see through them, so you have to avoid them. You can spot them ahead at up to 50 miles in medium-level flight, and at 30 miles from low level, so at your customary 240 knots you have about seven minutes to do something about a weather problem 30 miles ahead.

You also have to face the certainty that at some time in your navigation exercises, you are going to lose your way. If you do not, your instructor will deliberately make you lose your bearings. Later in your training you will be bounced by enemy aircraft, and you will have to divert from the planned course in order to deal with the threat. Regaining your course after you have lost track of where you should be is a vital skill. The detailed study of the route which you carried out on the previous evening is about to prove its value.

All you need to do, then, is check out the aircraft, take off, and set yourself up so that you fly wings level over the start point on the heading for the first leg. You will have the bug set on to the heading, corrected for the forecast wind. Check against your map that you are at the right height and flying at the right airspeed, and, as you pass overhead the start point, start the watch. Check again the heading, altitude and airspeed, and that the watch is running (the post-HAT checks), and note the time when you need to be looking for the next event.

If you are lucky, you will see the first fix dead ahead. Some pilots miss the fix because they are so accurate they fly right over it. More likely, you will have been working on an inaccurate wind forecast, and you will find you have been blown a few degrees off track. Keep flying the aircraft, and keep looking out, but be prepared for some more mental arithmetic. You need to fly the standard closing angle to regain your track. Estimate, if possible from the map, how many miles off track you were. Turn 15 degrees towards the track. (It is, in fact, 60 degrees divided by your true airspeed in nm per minute; in the Tucano's case four.) Hold the heading for as many minutes as you were miles off track. Turn back through 30 degrees on to the planned heading, and correct for the newly estimated wind, to avoid being blown off course again. No, it is not easy, but remember you have rehearsed it over and over again in the ground school and in the simulator, and you will have tested yourself and your friends on the course on all these mental calculations, over and over again.

Alternatively, if you have enough ground features you can follow them on the map, and fly along a 'funnel' feature – a river or road or railway line that intercepts your planned track – until you regain that track. Now adjust your heading to avoid repeating the inaccuracy.

It is not, clearly, much use sending a military pilot to work if he has to wait until the weather, and therefore the visibility, is fine. So unlike the private pilot, the military student must cover the full range of instrument flying, to the standard where he can fly confidently on civilian airways. The syllabus includes, naturally, navigating on instruments.

The student pilot in the Tucano has two primary navigation instruments – the horizontal situation indicator, and the relative magnetic indicator. He needs a third to interpret them – the customary sharp and agile mind.

The Tucano navigation system has access to two beacon systems in the UK: the civilian VOR system, and the military Tactical Navigation System, TACAN. The beacons are marked on the map, and as long as the student studies them before a sortie, and

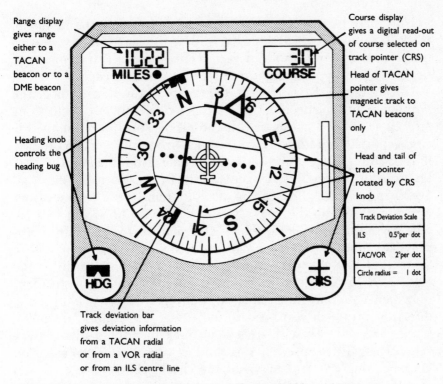

Range display gives range either to a TACAN beacon or to a DME beacon

Course display gives a digital read-out of course selected on track pointer (CRS)

Head of TACAN pointer gives magnetic track to TACAN beacons only

Heading knob controls the heading bug

Head and tail of track pointer rotated by CRS knob

| Track Deviation Scale | |
| --- | --- |
| ILS | 0.5°per dot |
| TAC/VOR | 2°per dot |
| Circle radius = | 1 dot |

Track deviation bar gives deviation information from a TACAN radial or from a VOR radial or from an ILS centre line

*Fig. 10* The Tucano's horizontal situation indicator (HSI) carries most of the information needed for accurate radio navigation

knows their Morse code identification signals, he should have no difficulty in locating his position, and in flying to another position. Once he has tuned to the beacon, and checked its identification, he can fly comfortably to any new position, so long as he can work a little recommended topographical calculation.

The becaons work on a system of 'radials' and distances. The needle points directly to the selected beacon, and if you fly towards the point of the needle, that is towards the beacon, you would be flying along a radial. As you fly, a small box in the corner of the display tells you know how far you still have to go to reach the beacon. Naturally, the occasion is rare when you want to fly directly along any radial, except perhaps to return to your home base. Usually, you need to fly towards a position offset from a beacon. But, in the course of preparing your map, you will have drawn a diagram of the radials and distances so that you can read off the position you want to fly to.

Now here is the somewhat novel way of finding the magnetic track to follow to reach your fix. Follow the diagram to stay with the reasoning. First, think of your HSI as a chart. It happens to be circular, but you can ignore that. Think of the beacon, whether TACAN or VOR, as lying in the centre of the chart. Ignore the pointed half of the needle; just concentrate on the 'rear' half. Your aircraft is located at the tail of the needle, on the radius of the circle, and that radius is your range from the beacon. In the illustration you are on radial 190, 30 miles from the beacon. You know from your map that you want to fly to a position on radial 80/20 miles from the beacon. In your mind's eye imagine that position drawn on the HSI. Now visualise the line from 190/30, where you are, to 80/20, where you plan to fly to. With a few practice tries, it is quite easy to do. Finally, in your imagination move that line sideways until it runs through the centre of the HSI. Now, by reading direction on the radius of the instrument to which your imaginary line is pointing, you can estimate the direction in which you need to fly. It is your required magnetic track. Are you still with it? Then adjust that track to compensate for the drift caused by the wind as you know it, to give you your heading. Fly it. Carry out the checks. Look out. And you should, by some miracle, arrive at your planned radio navigation fix.

At times, you will need to fly to a position further from the beacon than you are at present, and that brings an additional requirement into play. This time the greater distance – that of your planned fix – goes on to the outer radius as the main range. You need to assess your own range as a proportion of it, to give your position along the relevant half of the needle. Again, visualise the line between the two positions, transpose it to form a parallel line through the centre of the display, read off the heading where that line intersects the outer circumference to give your track, adjust for drift, and fly the heading. At 240 knots.

It is known as point-to-point navigation, and is a useful technique, especially when you have your head down in the cockpit, with an obscure visor fitted to your helmet to prevent you from seeing outside, and you are flying the aircraft with sole reference to the instruments. Small wonder that some students find it difficult to keep up with the learning load in the advanced stages of this course.

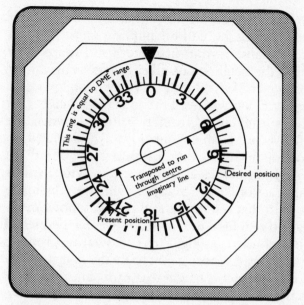

You are 220/30 from
the beacon
You wish to be 090/30
Turn to track 065°

*Fig. 11* Point-to-point navigation gives a quick picture of the heading
required to fly to a new position, using your distance and heading
from a beacon, and a little sharp mental calculation

This is not the full story of radio-aids navigation, and there is
a wide range of procedures, instruments, and systems that you need
to master. You are by now, however, achieving some command of
the aircraft and of the basic flying skills, visual and on instruments,
at medium level in free airspace, and on the airways.

Now you have to apply those skills, including the demanding art
of visual navigation, a new and even more exciting environment. It
will come as a treat for the genuinely enthusiastic student who
relishes a challenge. It is low flying.

As the *Student Guide* says, 'Modern radar systems can see
aircraft operating in all but the lowest airspace. Therefore aircraft
can expect to penetrate enemy defences only if they fly at extremely
low altitude.' Low altitude in war can be practically unmeasurable,
and only the pilot knows whether he is flying too low to be safe.
Low altitude in peace is rather more limited, by consideration for
the population at large and for livestock, so pilots at this stage in
the course are restricted to 250 ft dual and 500 ft solo. And
much as the general population believes otherwise, students and
instructors alike do their best to avoid upsetting both people and
animals. They know that their freedom to carry out low-flying

exercises depends on the tolerance of the population, and they do not want to sacrifice the confidence of the public.

Low flying is not easy, and in your instructor's introduction he will demonstrate what the heights look like, in a pass over your airfield at 500 ft and one at 250 ft. In that sortie you are expected to absorb the information you will need to judge those heights for yourself during later sorties away from the airfield, when the altimeter information is unreliable, and anyway you need to keep a constant lookout outside the cockpit. Your ability to maintain accurate height at low level will be a key factor in your success and eventual selection. Instructors, enjoying the advantage of years of experience in this activity, know precisely how low is low. The student has no real measure, and can become perplexed at trying to maintain a consistent height over undulating ground.

In the course of this lesson, we are going to fly the first two legs of a triangle at 500 ft. The brief is straightforward. The instructor will look after the navigation, and I am to fly the aircraft, learning to look after it at low level, and trying to maintain a constant speed and height. The route will take us out from the airfield on 240 degrees, turning at a clear waypoint, then we shall fly north along the eastern edge of the Pennines to a second waypoint. From there we will turn for home and at the same time climb to height to carry out the second part of the sortie, aerobatics at altitude.

By now I have flown a lot of circuits, and have got used to the behaviour of the aircraft, and the working of its systems. I am also sufficiently competent and trusted to sign out the aircraft, check it, get the clearances, taxi, and line it up for take-off. It is a fundamental truth of the natural flyer that he or she enjoys every item in the process. However many times you have done it before, the adrenalin starts to flow as you button up your buoyancy vest, check your gloves, helmet, and map, and initial the sheets and logs to take possession of the aircraft. The adrenalin flow increases dramatically as you taxi out to the holding point. The aircraft tries to run faster than you are allowed to let it. You steel yourself to rein it back in. Then it is time to let it fly, and that great surge of enjoyment starts as you release the brakes to roll, and at 75 knots you are flying again. It is what you were meant to do.

'Stay below the level of the chimneys. That's a good guide to 250 ft.'

From the rear seat the forgotten disembodied voice offers that startling guidance. The chimneys to which the instructor refers are part of the local power station. They stand like twin towers of Ilium, and if you were to follow all the instruction you received in the elementary phases of your flying career, you would avoid them by huge margins of height and lateral space. But this is grown-up flying, with new rules and unexpected liberalities allowed. 'That's about 250 ft, just below the top of the chimneys.' The reassuring command indicates no anxiety about keeping a safe distance from the chimneys, and they flash by, seemingly astonishingly close, though in reality you have to leave them at least 250 ft distant.

The instructor remains untroubled, so I assume we achieved at least that much separation.

'Stay at this height.' You push the nose down. 'That's about right.'

The aircraft seems recklessly close to the ground, especially when you take your eyes off the outside world to scan the instruments. The speed is 260 knots indicated; more than you expected, and more than is required. You are looking for 240 knots, so ease back the throttle with gentle pressure.

'Watch your height.' I was evidently drifting low while watching for the speed to come right. Somewhere in the back of the brain comes the recognition that I shall have to work out these details at much faster rates, checking and rechecking against the instruments, but without taking my eyes off the main business of flying by looking out at the outside world.

'Watch your height.'

The instructor still seems to have forgotten that at this low level, a student finds it extremely difficult to read his height. The contours are almost impossible to define as you pass close to them. If you were walking in these hills you would see the ups and downs unfolding in front of you. If you were flying in an airliner at 30,000 ft you would see nothing of the undulations, except in the most mountainous country, but you would not have to worry about following them either. Somewhere between, at say 500 ft, you have only a hazy idea that the land is changing in front of you, and by the time you read the ups and downs you have passed over them. You do not have to follow them with geometric rigidity; that would be both uncomfortable and inefficient. But you do need to fly at the correct average height, out of the way of defensive firepower and detection, and for that you need to fly a smooth course which evens out the bumps, but follows the general lie of the land. And you have to navigate at the same time.

It gives the new student the same old familiar problem of excessive workload.

The skill will come with experience, but in these early stages you almost always get it wrong, flying too low over the hills, and drifting high across the valleys. You have to keep your eyes flashing forwards, and to the sides, and down below, while keeping a sharp lookout for other aircraft. We fly over the reservoir where the Dambusters trained to drop Barnes Wallis's bouncing bombs. Their height, unbelievably, was 50 ft, and they flew at night. The drowned village in the bottom of the lake is exposed by the lack of summer rain. It is a gaunt and beautiful sight. A Chipmunk flies up the other side of the valley, its pilot also looking at the ruins. My instructor is indulgent, and lets me enjoy the free flying, a welcome relaxation from the tough tasks of learning. There is a gentle reminder as I fly too low over a ridge ahead. Ridges are a problem for the fighter pilot, even when he is fully experienced. If you follow the contour up to the ridge you will be climbing over its edge, and zooming up into airspace far too high above the valley beyond. You need to prepare to cross a ridge, climbing early as you approach it so that you can start to descend just before you clip its edge. That way, you will go low into the valley beyond as early as possible, out of the way of anti-aircraft defences. So climb, climb, climb, then push down over the edge. Few things are more exhilarating; we are flying at speeds and heights twice as fast and half as high as we have seen before, with the instructor deliberately letting me enjoy myself.

But the fun has to end, and we turn for the third leg of the sortie, to climb to height, avoid the airways, and prepare for some aerobatics.

Aerobatics is one of the items that sorts out the natural fighter pilot from the rest. There are other vital attributes to master and we shall see them all as we progress through the course, but if a pilot cannot handle aerobatics, he will not be able to cope with combat flying. If you have been through the EFTS or UAS system, you will have learned basic aerobatics. If you have come directly to the basic school, you will have to learn them from scratch on the Tucano. For the student who can handle the big machine, that may be no great disadvantage. At least he will have an abundance of power to carry him through the loops. And since the loops are necessarily bigger in the more powerful aircraft, he might even survive with less tendency to air sickness.

Since we have done some aerobatics before, our instructor lets us demonstrate our abilities on this familiarisation flight. First the climb to height. At 10,000 ft we are way above the clouds, and there is not much of an horizon. But the aircraft settles comfortably on 60 per cent power, and we try to demonstrate a steep turn in either direction. The first one is to the left. Most pilots, given a choice, turn to the left; it is a predictability that German pilots reportedly noted and used to their advantage in the First World War. Stick over, and gently pull back. The nose starts to describe its elegant way round the horizon. It starts to go down, so add a little power. It is surprisingly easy, and brings a word of appreciation into the helmet. Up here in this fabulous world you had momentarily forgotten about the instructor. 'Well done. Keep that going. Very nice.'

Keeping a flicking eye scanning the horizontal situation indicator, I roll the aircraft out level on the original westerly heading, and check that the height is still 10,000 ft. We have lost no more than 50 ft or so, so ease it back up gently.

'I'd like to try one to the right.'

'Go ahead.'

The movement is less natural, rather like a tennis backhand shot. Pull the stick outwards and ease it back. Go for 45 degrees, and look out. Keep the nose on the horizon. Put on a little more power. Then, wait for it, watch the HSI, then just roll out wings level and carefully take the power off at the same time. Not so accurate as the turn to the left, but good enough for an early flight.

'Try a stall.'

The inevitable checks have to be carried out, a sort of religious credo that has to be recited article-by-article, almost as a penance before we can allow ourselves to start the manoeuvre itself. Height: adequate at 10,000 ft. Airframe: no flap, gear up, as required for this exercise, or just 'clean' in the shorthand of the flying world. Security: no loose articles, canopy locked, seat-belts tight. Engine: check temperatures and pressures, and fuel. Location: away from controlled airspace and not over built-up areas or an active airfield.

Lookout: make a full 360-degree turn to look down below us, and level, and up above, to make sure that no other aircraft is likely to be inconvenienced by our stalling exercise. That turn is almost as much fun as any other part of flying. You can put the power on, dip the wing, and pull the aircraft round as though the wingtip were dug into a conical hole in the sky, and pivot – tight and fast, like an acrobat. Then level the wings and go straight into the stall. You have done it all before so you can feel comfortable about it. You know the aircraft is going to stop flying, and there could be an uncomfortable moment as you try to recover, but we are committed, so pull back the throttle to reduce power. The aircraft, clean, cruises resolutely on. It is, as they say in aerodynamics, a 'slippery' aircraft, and reluctant to slow down. A touch of airbrake, and if you press the stick firmly back to keep the nose up, it helps to reduce the speed, until the aircraft slumps and gently sags. It does have a few vices, which the test pilots have uncovered in their acceptance testing, but it stalls in a well-behaved manner, with no wing-drop or other disconcerting habits, and advancing the throttle is enough to get it flying again.

Determined to prove even at this early stage in the course that you are a born fighter-pilot, you are anxious to show off your aerobatics. You have heard that they like spirited flying, 'punchy' flying as some instructors say. It is true that they like somebody who can master the aircraft, and they look with caution at a student who is terrified of it. Many students are naturally sensitive at first in the unfamiliar machine, simply because they do not know what they are handling. But the sooner they come to terms with mastering the aircraft, the sooner the instructor can gain his own confidence in them. It is not the only attribute that they are looking for, so you will have to demonstrate a great deal more than the ability to throw an aircraft about the sky, but at least you will get some kind of reputation in the instructor's room for wanting to get on with the job of flying.

OK. Aerobatics. Carry out the abbreviated checks, then you can start. You plan to begin with an aileron roll to the left.

'Just raise the nose and push the stick over.'

I pull up the nose a few degrees, then gently apply left stick. The Tucano rolls, somewhere between active and leisurely, and I knew I had not done enough. As the world swivelled in front of me, I became entranced by it, and as it came upright, I was late stopping the roll, and struggled to get the wings back to level without looking too inept.

'I'd like to try another one, to the right. And I will try harder.'

'OK, Go ahead.'

Raise the nose again, and pull the stick hard to the right, with real pressure. It is ridiculously, juvenilely liberating. To the right the puffball clouds. Below – irrelevantly far below – the khaki earth, and ahead and all around the blueness of this medium in which we operate. And here we are, turning in it like astronauts, with no thought for the realities of the mundane uni-directional world which ordinary people inhabit. Over, and upside down, and the world swivels ahead with extraordinary speed, and comes upright again, so centre the stick with a flick, and stop the roll. You know you have done well.

'I'll try a slow roll, sir, if that's all right.'

The instructor seems to be taking the treatment without protest. He must enjoy flying like this. Or he regards it as his duty to suffer it in silence and throw me off the course at the later debriefing.

I carry out the checks again, abbreviated to cover the height, engine condition, and lookout and location, because we already have the other items under control, then straight into a slow roll. Very different, this.

The aircraft is not much help. You find yourself fighting against it, as well as dealing with the complicated actions you need to keep the manoeuvre going. Nose up a little, then stick gently over. The aircraft rolls on to a knife-edge, with one wing pointing down, the other vertically up. If you were to continue to hold it like that, the nose would now begin to drop, so you need to apply some top rudder. Fine. But keep the stick over and the aircraft will turn on to its back. Now you need to straighten the rudder, so adjust your feet to an even position. It is not easy, when you are hanging upside down in the straps and your feet are trying to fall off the pedals earthwards. And if you hold the aircraft inverted like that, the nose will come down and you will stand a chance of entering the second half of a loop, so you need to push the stick forward and away from yourself to keep the nose up. You also have to keep the stick over, so that you continue to roll and come up to the other side. And now you will need the opposite top rudder to stop the nose from slipping down again, and begin to bring the stick back. And as you come upright, you can centralise the rudder with your boots, and ease back the stick fully to bring you into level flight. It is like circling your hands over your head and stomach in opposite directions – in triplicate.

Grateful to be upright and at least in some shape, you offer to go for the opposite slow roll, and try to keep it all in good order. Nose up, and stick over to the right. Left rudder. Now you are coming inverted, so stick away from you and centralise the rudder. Now you are hanging in your straps, your bottom off the seat and your thighs taking the strain, and your feet are coming up towards your chin, off the pedals. You feel helpless, and hang on to the stick as your only support with the real world, pulling it towards you, which is precisely the opposite of what you want. Push it away, and maintain the pressure to the right to continue the roll. The aircraft rolls on to its wing and you remember to apply top rudder, and it keeps coming round, and rolls out level, so centralise everything. Somewhere in the middle of the roll, you have lost all sense of where you are, like a child in the middle of a somersault in a playground, and you come out of it amazed that you can recover your orientation and your familiarity with the real world.

But you cannot afford to let the fun seduce you. There are more serious aerobatics to attempt in this new aircraft. Time to demonstrate your barrel roll.

'Off you go then. Just dive it to the right and then climb and roll it to the left.'

Power on, and dive off to the right. The speed builds up rapidly. Now pull back, and centralise the stick, and the view of the earth instantly changes to a big blue picture of the sky, unnervingly complete, with no features to help you to orient yourself. For a few moments, you are flying on faith and recent memory-references. Hold the stick back to maintain the loop, and begin to press it to the left. Somewhere under your left nostril the brown earth arrives again. If you had to make a confession, you would confess to not knowing quite where you were, but if you hold it like that, before you have time to think through the problem you are diving down towards the earth and pulling the nose up and levelling the wings to bring you back to straight and level flight. Not too fast now. Just keep the pressure on, and watch the height and direction so that you do not come out too low or on the wrong heading.

But you know you had lost it in the final few seconds, and the aircraft had dished out shallow at the bottom. Damn. You could lose your fighter pilot career on the strength of failures like that. There is only one way to do it, and that is to concentrate on the correct procedure and go out and practise it when you finally get permission to go solo.

You confess: 'That wasn't very accurate. I'd like to try another, to the right this time.'

'Off you go then.'

Dive down to the left, and pull up. When the canopy fills with blue, ease the stick to the right, and keep the aircraft rolling and looping. Look for the ground, and as we come near to our starting point gently relax the pull on the stick to level out and finally ease off the roll to bring the wings straight.

Magic! You got one.

Suddenly you feel good, and ambitious. 'I'll try a vertical roll, please.'

'When you are ready.'

The vertical roll looks and sounds easy. Just point the aircraft vertically upwards, and push the stick hard over to the left or right. The aircraft will roll as it climbs. Watch for the pattern of the clouds or the horizon to resume its original shape, then stop the roll.

It is not as easy as that. First, put on the power, and pull back on the stick to start the climb. The clouds disappear, and blue sky fills the canopy. The trouble with blue sky is that it offers few reference points, so you have no way of knowing when you are pointing the nose vertically. Look out of the side of the canopy instead, and you will have a horizon of sorts to refer to. Ease off the pull on the stick when you think you are going straight up perpendicular to the horizon. You ought to check the speed now, but you are too intent on looking out. And you need to get on with the roll before you run out of climbing energy.

Push the stick over left. The horizon begins to spin. You are meant to look for a reference point off the wing before you start the roll, but in your haste to get the manoeuvre going you missed that, and now you find that all the clouds look precisely the same. Anyway, not to worry; you have started the roll, and as you think you have gone through 360 degrees, centre the stick to stop rolling.

Now what? You have expended virtually all your energy, and you are pointing upwards. The choices are, mainly, to push the stick over to the side and fly out left or right under control, or to pull back on the stick and come out in the second half of a loop. Pull back. Again, nothing is visible until the horizon begins to appear above your eyebrows. By this time you are becoming completely disoriented. You have lost all sense of direction, and your sense of altitude has deserted you. You seem to be high enough above the earth for safety, and that unforgiving earth is beginning to fill the cockpit canopy. You could hold the stick back, and pull through the loop until you begin to feel the buffet. Or you can half-roll the aircraft. Try that. Miraculously, the aircraft simply rights itself. You pick it up, and fly out straight and level. But you are travelling in no direction that you ever remembered, and the world has become totally unfamiliar. It will inevitably have done so, unless you made your originally vertical roll through exactly 360 degrees.

Check the height: 200 ft below your 10,000. You need to start to think in three dimensions, and keep your wits about you.

The instructor seems encouraged. 'Let's try something more demanding.'

'I'll try a half Cuban, sir.'

'Good. Off you go then.'

Nose down and gently to full power. Speed rising, and smartly pull up the nose. The g force tugs at your arms and drags your cheeks down. The helmet takes on its familiar excess weight. Your stomach feels as if it is trying to exit your body rearwards. Tense your muscles – neck, stomach, and shoulders. The aircraft is looping now, up and over. The sky is deep blue, and there are no reference points. Just hold the stick central, and look up. You can see your own eyebrows. Then the earth, inverted, brown in the distance. Hold the loop on. Get the nose coming well down. Do you remember your heading when you went into the manoeuvre? Of course you don't. You forgot to check it. You should have the reciprocal firmly in your mind so that you know what direction you are coming out in. Never mind. Too late to worry now. Just hold on the loop. Don't be tempted to roll out too early. Just when you think you are about to pull the nose through the vertical, push the stick over. The Tucano rolls left like a top. Stop the roll. Adjust to correct the slight error. Now you are flying safely down the hill and you can come out of the dive in a smooth curve, and ease off the power.

'And again for the other half, sir?'

You feel it is going well, and you are beginning to enjoy yourself. Power on again. Check the heading. We are on 60 degrees, and we have gone down to 9,600 ft. Remember the figures: 9,600, and the reciprocal is . . . Damn. Your brain is giving up. Pull back. It comes to you: 240 degrees. Remember it. Climb with wings level. Hold it. Keep pulling. Not too tight. Slowing over the top. Look up. See the horizon coming down from over your head. Hold it. Hold everything. Keep it like that, ease off the power, and when the earth fills the canopy pull it into a half-roll. Check the speed. Make sure he knows you are checking it. Say it out loud: '250 degrees, and we lost 100 ft or so in the dive-out.' Correct that quickly to 240 degrees and 9,600 ft.

'Quite good that. You seem to enjoy your aerobatics.'

Enjoy it! It's the whole point of flying. It is the most exciting, masterly, lordly, liberating, anti-mundane activity known. It will not be, at least in its purely aerobatic form, particularly relevant to the job of being a fighter pilot, but if you can cope with flying upside down, and you actually enjoy it, when the g is tearing at you and you are beginning to feel thoroughly airsick, and through all of that you can maintain your orientation and keep control of the aircraft, you might just make it as a fast-jet pilot.

There is more to it, however, than the sense of elation induced by high-level aerobatics. And another aspect of your skill is about to be put to the test. Suddenly the stick comes back and the revolutions drop. Your heart sinks at the same time. You can feel the dreaded 'emergency' coming on.

'You have an engine failure. How are you going to deal with it?'

Every pilot, time after time in the course of his training, and throughout his career after it, is confronted by simulated emergency after simulated emergency. Each one, and there are several different ones, from engine failure on take-off, to engine fire, to engine failure at altitude, to birdstrike with loss of canopy, is dealt with differently. And as you go through your flying career each new aircraft that you fly has a different set of emergency procedures. You have an opportunity to practise them in the simulator, and you are given time to learn the procedure off by heart. But none of that is the same as carrying out the procedure without warning, and in an aircraft in flight. It is misery, but it shows how well you can cope with the unexpected.

The throttle comes back, operated by an unseen hand in the rear cockpit. The engine falls to near zero revolutions: not quite zero, in this aircraft, but that is no help. The engine note falls away. You are alone with your panic. First, get the speed right, and return the aircraft to straight and level flight. Now plan the descent. You practised it in the Bulldog, or the Chipmunk, or the local club aeroplane, and in the simulator, but the 'emergency' always comes as a shock.

The aircraft is beginning to descend, and the time available is reducing as fast as the number of checks you have to make appears to be growing. Choose a suitable field, and work out the way you intend to fly your final approach. Set up your high key position. The map of the descent in your mind begins to get confused with the picture you see below you. Check the aircraft to identify the fault. Fuel, electrics, all the indications. No result. Call your intentions. Remember you have to carry out only 'touch' drills. You are approaching your critical height. And still turning. Now go for the low key position. Christ, you must have missed something out. You know you have. Gear. Touch the undercarriage handle and the other finals checks. And watch the height. Your minimum for training is 500 ft. You are nearly there. You turn on to finals, luckily rolling out at the beginning of the field; lucky because you were not really in control. But it worked. Apply power and raise the nose. Remember the gear up. And you are climbing away into the beautiful blue.

'And if you would fly us back to the airfield, please.'

Where is the airfield? Panic. Relax. Relax! You have almost passed this test. You know you have. Now if you keep your brain together you might get away with it.

A cool head in a crisis is the mark of every experienced pilot, but it is the ability to stay composed and function under extreme stress that distinguishes the fighter pilot *par excellence*. Flying fighters, and training to fly fighters, is a life of relentless pressure. In the course of a single training sortie, decision follows decision, with no relief from the pressure. It is not hobby flying; it is not relaxing. It is hard, challenging, and tiring. As the size and speed of the aircraft increases, at each successive stage in training, the level of challenge rises, as does the speed of response the student needs to deal with it. Later in the pilot's training, and perhaps even in combat itself, a new range of pressures entirely will be added to the requirement. Naturally, nobody is expected to pick up the skills of flying by magic. The training is progressive and continuous, and many students do survive it and go forward into fast-jet flying. But those students need two distinct qualities, as well as a wide range of less definable ones. They need, first, the ability to cope with this extreme and continuing pressure, to solve difficult problems one after another without folding or freezing or forgetting what they are supposed to be doing. They need, secondly, the ability to keep up with events. The student who does not stay in touch with the rapid development of a training flight will not be able to think clearly in the pressure of a fast-jet combat sortie.

To achieve that level of skill, the basic requirement, and the one that will get the student over almost all of his hurdles and round his blocks, is motivation. Time and again the instructors will tell you that motivation is the key to success. They do not expect perfect flying all the time. They do look for a student's determination to overcome the obstacles. If they see evidence of that determination, they are more than willing to help the student through the difficult patches.

If, at the end of the course, the student is clearly not going to be able to cope with the pressures and demands of the fast-jet world, his instructors will 'stream' him into another branch of flying. Streaming is the uncompromising process by which students are assigned to their future careers, or at least to the next stage on route to those careers. Streaming takes place formally at the end of the course, but the instructors will have arrived at a provisional decision about all their students several days, or in some cases even weeks, earlier.

Some students will have been taken off flying already, and will almost certainly have left the basic flying school by this time. Some of them will have pulled out of fixed-wing flying altogether, and opted for a career in helicopters. For the rest there are two possible courses. One is in a branch of flying that will suit the pilot with a lot of steady courage – multi-engined aircraft. That is not necessarily a second-best option. It can call for just as much courage, and flying skill, and airmanship, as any other branch of flying. It might involve transport aircraft, air-to-air refuelling, or airborne surveillance, including airborne early warning. One recent student was assessed as lacking the aptitude for fast-jet flying, and could not assimilate the learning in the time available for the course. He was assigned to multi-engined training, and a career that promised none of the excitement of fast jets. The slower pace of the multi-engined world worked for him, and he found a niche flying Hercules transport aircraft, but not in a routine environment. His job was delivering Special Forces into enemy territory, which was hardly a second-rate flying job, and was not in the least boring. Many of the students who are streamed away from fast-jet flying into the multi-engined world are relieved to see the end of their fast-jet prospects. Enough for them of the low-level, high-pressure, brief sortie out-and-back-at-low-level variety of aviation. They can go into a less hectic profession, with more travel, more time in the cockpit, and in many ways as much challenge and variety.

But for most students, the aim is the same as it was at the start of the courses – the combat jet. And for those who have succeeded in satisfying the examiners, the end of propeller-aircraft flying is in sight. They are looking towards their first jet, and there is only one place where they can learn that skill – RAF Valley. A short leave, and they will move to North Wales, for their first acquaintance with the Hawk, and flying at almost twice the speed of anything they have flown before.

# 7

# Pilot, Fast Jet

You have been selected for training for what is known technically as Group 1, Phase 2. That somewhat bland categorisation fails completely to describe the reality of your next phase of training, popularly known as Pilot, Fast Jet. You are going to RAF Valley, to learn to fly the Hawk.

As the *Student Guide* says: 'The Hawk is a high-performance aircraft and you will find that the pace of events is somewhat faster than that to which you have been accustomed. However, once you have learned to cope with the more advanced airmanship requirements, you will find that you will soon start to adapt to the new pace and should enjoy the course flying.'

'Somewhat faster than that to which you have been accustomed' is, in fact, a normal operating speed of 420 knots, as against the Tucano's normal operating speed of 240 knots. The difference is startling. At RAF Valley the student has to learn to cope with it.

But first there is ground school. Almost universally, pilots hate ground school. Here it lasts for eight weeks, and covers aerodynamics, aviation medicine, avionics and flight instruments, combat survival, meteorology, pilot navigation, technical, electronic warfare, and weapons.

The aviation medicine element is covered at RAF North Luffenham, and ensures that the student can cope with decompression. Combat survival takes place in the open air. Students are equipped with a parachute and a dinghy, just as they would be if they ejected from the aircraft in anger. From the parachute they are expected to make a shelter; from the dinghy they must fashion a bed. They are supplied with items such as dead rabbits, which, if they want to eat at all, they will skin, clean and cook themselves. 'Living like that makes you very tired, and you slow down badly, and it is not for the squeamish,' a student said.

After combat survival the return to RAF Valley, even for more ground school, is welcome. The ground school academic subjects are learned through a self-teaching package which enables the student to progress at his own pace. If he learns each item rapidly he can go on to the next element in the course. If he is slow, he puts in more hours in the evenings, and the job takes longer. Later on, the course becomes intermingled with simulator training and with flying itself. At various critical points in the course the student must pass a certain ground school academic test before he can go on with the next of his simulator flights, and later with the next part of the course in the air. There is no percentage pass mark. The material is in the course because the student is expected to know it. If he does not know it – all of it – he does it again. If he still does not know it he can be back-coursed. And if he cannot master it at all in a reasonable time, he might fail the course altogether.

Just as in the other parts of training, each ground school subject is set out with the objective, the relevant text, a set of self-assessed questions, and the answers to those questions.

At this level, the information is becoming relatively advanced. 'Aerodynamics and aircraft performance' (Group 1, advanced) is a good example of the level of learning that the fast-jet pilot must achieve. It covers the Aerodynamic Characteristics of the Hawk, Compressible Flow, Shock Wave Formation on an Aerofoil, Effect of Compressibility on Lift, and Effect of Compressibility on Drag.

Take Shock Wave Formation on an Aerofoil. The objective states: 'After you have read this chapter you will be able to a) identify Mach numbers for particular arrangements of shock waves on a thin aerofoil at zero angle of attack; b) Identify angles of attack for particular arrangements of shock waves on a thin aerofoil at constant Mach number; c) State the effects of shock wave formation on the boundary layer.'

And from the text: 'Fig. 2:1 shows us a typical aerofoil at a speed slightly higher than M CRIT. The acceleration over the upper surface has produced an ML of 1 where the camber is greatest. This gives a small area of supersonic flow which will then expand downstream as speed increases. As it does so it meets small pressure waves from the rear of the aerofoil (which is still subsonic). These pressure waves are unable to advance up-stream into the supersonic regions and they therefore coalesce to form a shock wave which terminates the supersonic region. Increasing the Mach number causes the supersonic region to increase in size both upstream and downstream, while the shock moves rearwards and becomes more oblique. At about MFS=0.95 the shock reaches the trailing edge.'

And the self-assessed questions relating to that text: 'Sketch typical shock wave patterns for a thin symmetrical bi-convex aerofoil of 8 per cent Thickness/Cord ratio at zero angle of attack in a high speed airflow at the following Mach numbers: a) CRIT; b) M FS=0.85; c) M FS=1.01.'

By the time he has absorbed that information, to the level where he can answer all the related questions without exception or error, the student is moving some way towards the equivalent of a degree standard in aeronautics. He is also becoming desperate for his next excursion into flying.

Before the aircraft itself, however, there are at least six exercises to complete in the simulator. If your instructor believes that more than the six 'simexes' are necessary, he will provide more. And if you are enthusiastic enough to want to practise your cockpit drills you can ask for more. The simulator staff are always willing to accommodate a keen student. In any case, just as you have to pass the academic tests before you can go on to the simulator, you certainly have to pass the relevant simexes before you can go on to the next block of flying exercises.

So put on your flying kit, helmet, and life vest, and climb into the simulator. It is the same as the Hawk cockpit, except that it has no outside view. At this stage in the training there are no visual images, although the United States Navy in its version of the Hawk will train extensively on full visual simulators. Nor does it have full motion simulation, though it does bump and lurch in response to serious inputs such as heavy landings. Strap yourself in, and the instructor will talk you through the procedures, from start-up through take-off to shut-down and even ejection. Then the canopy comes down over you and blots out all vision, leaving only a ghostly translucent glare, with the air conditioning whining away and sounding just like jet noise. The simulator is not for the claustrophobic.

Now you can begin to 'fly' the machine. The communication in the headset inside your helmet is with the instructor. At this stage in the course, the emphasis is on your ability to cope with the many emergencies which might afflict the Hawk, although along the way the student practises handling the aircraft on instruments alone, and rehearses the innumerable checks that any aircraft demands, most of which, as always in the military environment, have to be learned by heart.

Basic handling, take-off procedure, climbing and levelling off, instrument descent procedure, before-landing checks and after-landing checks, all come in the course of the hour-long Simex 2.

Simex 3 repeats them and adds take-off technique, a climb from Runway 14 on a given radial, engine handling, and a precision radar approach to return to Runway 14.

In Simex 4, which, like all the others, lasts for an hour, failures and emergencies are added – start failure from no GTS or no rotation, radio failures, transmit button failure, loss of RT – the list of possibilities is limitless.

By the end of Simex 5 the student has covered two kinds of start failure, an instrument take-off and radial climb to FL 350, TACAN radial intercepts and orientation, oxygen and cabin pressure warnings, temperature malfunctions, smoke or fumes, undercarriage failure and emergency retraction, and emergency ground egress.

Failures covered in the sixth simulator hour include hydraulic systems, airbrake and trim malfunctions, and hydraulic failures at minimum landing speed; and in the instrument flying area you practise recovery by QGH (magnetic bearing) or TACAN, and precision approach radar.

In the course of the seventh hour the valve sticks open during the take-off run, and the take-off is aborted. The aircraft is restarted for an instrument take-off and radial climb, with pitot icing, electrical failures, generator and battery warnings, leading to standby instrument flying, with revision of hydraulics failures, recovery, and ejection.

In Simex 8 rpm overtrimming is covered, along with under-carriage malfunction after take-off, three forms of engine relight (immediate, cold unassisted, and cold assisted), oil and EOHT problems, engine seizure, forced landing, and barrier engagement. That is where, following a brake failure, you run off the end of the runway into an oversized tennis net.

Exercise 9 concentrates almost exclusively on emergencies, with a fire warning after engine start, high turbine gas temperature on the runway, engine icing, a start warning in flight, JPOHT, compressor surge, fire warning in the air, noxious fumes drill, forced landing, ejection drill, and manual bale-out drill.

Exercise 10, you are gratified to learn, is the last of this phase of the course. It reviews your command of a selection from the emergencies you have learned to deal with, together with engine failure on take-off, undercarriage unlocked, a fire warning, and a recovery related to whichever final emergency the instructor decides to throw at you.

Once you have passed Simex 6, you will be allowed to fly dual in the Hawk. But not until you have proved your ability to handle competently every one of those emergencies, and have passed the relevant critical points in the academic syllabus, are you permitted to fly solo.

It is worth putting the effort into the ground school and simulator, just for the sheer pleasure of flying the Hawk. It is one of the most successful small aircraft in the world, selected by air forces in several countries, and by the United States Navy as their advanced training aircraft.

The Hawk is a two-seat tandem aircraft, powered by a single Rolls-Royce/Turbomeca Adour engine of 5,700 lb thrust. It is reliable and free of vices, but is agile and manoeuvrable. It is not designed as a supersonic aircraft, although it will just exceed the speed of sound in a shallow dive. It is, however, a fighter pilot's aircraft, and in various advanced forms has been developed for several combat roles, including close air support, interdiction, reconnaissance, airspace denial, and anti-shipping operations. It is also the aircraft flown by the Red Arrows aerobatic display flying team.

In terms of performance it is, for the student at this stage of his learning, a revelation of an aircraft's true potential, compared with any of the propeller-powered aircraft he has flown previously. Take-off is not dissimilar to that of the Tucano. Apply full power against the brakes, release the brakes, and the Hawk rolls forward and picks up speed at a brisk rate. At about 90 knots ease the stick back to raise the nosewheel, and at 100 knots the aircraft lifts off. Fifteen seconds have elapsed since brake release, and you have travelled about 2,000 ft. The aircraft continues to accelerate rapidly, and you can settle it into a climb at 300 knots indicated, converting to Mach 0.7 as height is gained, and at that rate you will arrive at 30,000 ft in six minutes from brake release, or, if you go on climbing, 40,000 ft in less than four minutes more. If you are flying a transit route you begin the cruise at 20,000 ft, gradually increasing your altitude to 46,000 ft and your speed to 0.69 M, and that will give you a ferry range of about 1,400 nm or 2,400 km.

The cockpit is roomy, with a perfect all-round view through the single-piece canopy, and, after the basic flying training course, you will be familiar with the layout of the cockpit and the functions of most of the instruments. The only problem that curtails the career of some potential pilots is knee-room. Wearing an immersion suit, over a bunny suit or flying suit, the pilot is well padded around the bottom. This pushes him up and forward. The rudder pedals are adjustable for travel forwards and back, and the seat is adjustable up and down, but there is a limit, and pilots have to fit within an acceptable thigh length. If they exceed it, and have to make an ejection, they are likely to leave their kneecaps behind on the lower edge of the instrument panel, and that, as they say in aviation, could spoil their entire day.

The main difference between the Hawk and the Tucano, apart from the speed, is that the jet operates without the torque associated with propeller aircraft, and you can almost forget the actions of your feet which you learned when you had to compensate for torque changes as you increased or decreased your speed in the Tucano. The course at RAF Valley is, to a large extent, inevitably an extension of the course at the basic flying training level. Much of the flying is similar, but is re-learned to reinforce your ability and to extend your flying skills into the jet environment, particularly in adapting to the higher speed. Indeed much of the work of the instructor lies not in the area of teaching new material, but in that of fault analysis. The student spends much of his time developing a more advanced level of understanding of what he is doing, and learning to do it with refined skills.

The syllabus itself expresses this relative simplicity, and shows how much of the course is a repetition of what has gone before: aircraft familiarisation, effects of controls, stalling, circuits, practice forced landings, spinning, aerobatics, maximum rate turning, high level, instrument flying, introduction to low level, low-level navigation, high-level navigation, close formation, tactical formation, and night flying. Of these subjects only tactical formation flying will be entirely new to the student. Much of the rest will be reinforcement of existing skills, though at vastly increased speeds.

The first lesson, *Familiarisation*, is for most students a welcome return to flying. For some it can be intimidating to start afresh as a new boy in a new environment, and for others it becomes a trial, as the first flight after a period on the ground can produce airsickness.

After a thorough briefing and a confirmation of your swift and efficient command of the checks, the instructor taxies out, letting you take control for a short time. He demonstrates the take-off and climb. It is, in a word, breathtaking to find yourself powering in seconds to speeds and heights that in your previous aircraft had seemingly taken minutes. The instructor is enthusiastic. Your problem is staying confident that you will be able to cope with the aircraft at these speeds. At about 350 knots he lets you fly a large wingover, then tells you to go to 450 knots and fly another. If you like he will let you practise your basic aerobatics, helping you by calling your entry speeds, and the correct g, pattering you through the manoeuvres, since you are obviously a little rusty. You feel that you are subjecting the instructor to forces that will make him unwell, but he never seems to mind, and the instructors all seem to enjoy being with a student who is enthusiastic and flies with determination and spirit.

On the other hand, he will not mind either if on this first sortie you let him know that you are feeling sick. It happens to a lot of delicate stomachs after an extended ground period. But not to yours. You are beginning to appreciate the performance of the Hawk compared with your previous piston-powered aircraft. Roll it, left and right, and it responds instantly. Loop it, and it gains and sheds thousands of feet effortlessly. You begin to realise what power you are going to handle in your jet-flying career. There is no need to dive to store up momentum for a manoeuvre. You just build up the speed with the throttle, pull g, and perform.

Your stomach is still in good order, so the instructor lets you take the aircraft down for some low flying, first at 500 ft, then at 250 ft. That is even more exciting. You recall your first flight at 240 knots behind the engine of the Tucano. It was your first experience of high-speed flight. Then, gradually, you grew accustomed to the sensation. Now you are at nearly double the speed.

There is less buffet, but you need to keep your attention riveted on the landscape as it flashes towards and beneath you. 'Watch the speed,' the voice murmurs from down in the front cockpit. You glance down and read off the speed, somewhere near to 450 knots. Ease back the throttle. Too much, and the speed drops towards 400. Look ahead. Ease it forwards. Trim. Flying a jet really is different. Put in some turns, to skirt the villages. You are speechless, concentrating on the task of flying as well as you can, hoping to make a good impression on your new instructor, and enjoying the sheer ecstasy of this first familiarisation flight.

Your second flight, *Effects of Controls*, which if you are lucky could be later on that same day, extends the familiarisation process, and introduces you to more of the basic handling characteristics of the aircraft. This is your first working sortie, so you must begin to concentrate on the detail, but your instructor is careful not to overload you. All the confidence you built up on your first flight could easily be destroyed.

In this lesson you begin to learn to be responsible for the aircraft, going through the procedures at the operations desk, the safety equipment department, and the line hut, where you sign the aircraft out and later in again. You go through the external pre-flight check, which will soon be entirely your responsibility when you go solo. And you take responsibility for the vital brakes check as the aircraft begins to move. This time you follow through on the controls as your instructor demonstrates the take-off. Line up on the centreline with the nosewheel straight, apply the brakes, switch on the landing lamp, apply full power, check the engine indications, and release the brakes. That same high-powered take-off run. Watch the airspeed indicator and feel for the rudder to keep the aircraft straight. Gently apply a brake to straighten it, until after 50 knots the rudder becomes fully effective. At 90 knots ease back the stick to raise the nosewheel, and soon after that, at 120 knots, you can feel it fly off. The speed builds up rapidly. By 200 knots you need to have gear and flaps retracted, then you can lower the nose to 6 degrees nose-up to accelerate. When you have 350 knots raise the nose to 11 degrees nose-up and you will climb like a rocket. In no time you are at 10,000 ft, Flight Level 100, and the instructor levels out. You look out, carefully, behind you over your shoulders, and above you through the clear canopy, ostensibly to check for other aircraft in the airspace, in reality because you cannot resist admiring the majesty of the skyscape and the land far below, and your apparent dominance over it. You had better get used to it. There is work to be done, and not much time for sightseeing.

In Effects of Controls your instructor shows how powered controls are incredibly responsive, but when you take control you find you are jerky and twitchy on the stick. You need to smooth out your actions. You learn the sensitivity of the trim, and the need to watch the slip ball to make sure you have the aircraft in balance through all the speed changes. Then he lets you fly some manoeuvres, large wingovers, turns with 45 degrees angle of bank, which are none too effective, and tighter turns at 3 g with 70 degrees angle of bank. Again you are learning the difference in the jet. To turn a fast jet you roll the aircraft on to what seems like a knife-edge and pull g. The aircraft will not mind. If you try to turn by rolling on a gentle bank, it will go powering away in a near-straight line to the other end of the county.

Now select idle and try the airbrake. This is new, and interesting. It changes the pitch slightly, gives you a reassuring deceleration, and puts in a slight buffet. The airbrake could come in handy if you begin to get into trouble. It is time to carry out the checks (remember to do it regularly so that the instructor does not have to prompt you). This time it is FOEL (Fuel, Oxygen, Engine, Location). In a fast jet you can soon become disoriented and you need to know where you are.

And into some more aerobatics. First the instructor takes control and demonstrates, smoothly. A loop, half Cuban, an aileron roll, and a slow roll. 'Like to try those? You have control.' You go through the sequence, and he patters you through them. A bit better than your first Hawk lesson, but not nearly so smooth as his. But he has been flying the Hawk for a long time. He is quite pleased with your progress.

He flies a simulated circuit for you, demonstrating the circuit pattern, the crosswind landing technique, the minimum power setting of 70 per cent rpm for the approach, and the overshoot procedure. You take control and practise, in the safety of middle air, nowhere near to the ground. It is a long time since you flew a circuit, but the sequences and checks are coming back to you. You begin to hunger for more demanding flying, to exploit the potential of this challenging thoroughbred machine. But over-eagerness is the enemy of quality flying. You will have to be patient. You turn for base, to recover to the airfield, and at 10 miles out he takes control, flies a perfect circuit, and lands. You resent it slightly. He doesn't need the practice as much as you do. But you steel yourself to be patient. You like this instructor. He seems sympathetic, and he likes your spirited flying, and flies with spirit himself. You feel in good hands. There is always the possibility that an instructor and student can change if you don't get on with him, or he with you, and you don't want to lose him. You are building up a good relationship, and beginning to master the course. It is time for your working sorties to begin in earnest.

Throughout your training, *Stalling* has loomed large in your thinking. You plan never to stall an aircraft, but all good air forces and civilian training establishments insist on your practising the stall technique, so that you can recognise the symptoms of the developing stall, and know what to do to keep out of trouble. You need to have the recovery actions drilled into your brain.

The course on the Hawk is no different. The lesson, as ever, starts with the briefing. SABIRS is the new mnemonic. Speed: the aircraft decelerates slowly when clean, more rapidly during 'configuration' stalls, with the gear and flaps down. Attitude: as the aircraft decelerates the attitude for level flight increases. Buffet: occurs at about 135 knots clean. With gear and full flap selected there is noticeable configuration buffet, but it is different from pre-stall buffet, which starts at 105 knots. Instability: lateral instability can be controlled with ailerons, yaw instability with rudder. Rate of descent: a high sink rate develops. Stick position: the stick may be moved progressively fully aft. And there is one more point to watch for, that pitch oscillations may develop. (You can remember the mnemonic, but it is a bit of a struggle to remember what the mnemonic stands for.)

Fortunately the standard stall recovery is natural in this aircraft, unlike some, and all you have to do is push the stick forward, apply full power, and level the wings with aileron. In some aircraft you must level the wings with rudder, to correct the yaw which caused the wing to drop in the first place. It is an unnatural action, and often forgotten by the unwary. Stalling is anyway a tedious unnatural drill — 'unflying' the aircraft as opposed to flying it — and you are anxious to get this lesson over.

The pre-stalling checks are the same as ever, but fortunately in the Hawk you get rapidly to a suitable stalling height, unlike in your first aircraft with those interminable climbs. FOEL check first, which you are now expected to carry out every five minutes, followed by the old HASELL check, ending with the lookout turn, in which you decelerate, and roll the wings level at 160 knots, and then go straight into the stall. You call the symptoms as they occur. Remember SABIRS. Speed falling, Attitude changing as the nose comes up, there is the light Buffet, work the stick to control the Instability, we are descending at a rapid Rate, and the Stick is fully aft.

Recovering now . . . stick forward full power and stick back to bring us into a shallow climb. Back to 10,000 ft, and carry out the FOEL and HELL checks (the abbreviated HASELL) and carry out the stall all over again, four times, once in the approach configuration with gear and full flap selected, once with mid flap selected, once with full flap in a finals turn, and once flapless in a finals turn.

Finally, a change from stalling, as the instructor demonstrates the performance loss as you go beyond light buffet to moderate buffet, in a turn at 280 knots. He stresses the two main points of the lesson, that you cannot afford to pull buffet during your finals turn, or if you do you had better carry out the standard stall recovery and go round for another try. And that the best performance in this aircraft comes at the light buffet, so don't pull to the heavy buffet during aerobatics and tailchasing.

You wonder whether you can ever remember all the material you have learned about stalling in its manifold variety of forms.

There are even more numbers to remember in that other standard drill of the trainee pilot, *Circuits* – normal circuit, low-level circuit, flapless circuit, and the run-in and break. Each has its own set of numbers to be learned and applied, and in the Hawk the circuit is fast, so there is even less time to spare than there was in the Tucano. Still, flying accurate circuits is a vital consolidation of your skills, and develops confidence and sound airmanship, so get on with it. Prepare the lessons as well as you can. Drill the checks and performance figures into your mind. Eliminate as many of the worries as you can by means of good detailed planning, and fly accurately. At the Advanced School, the principles are just as they were on the UAS or EFTS and at the Basic School. It is just the speed with which they all come round that alters. And it just needs work and hard thinking to cope. At first, the instructor is flexible on the details, and tries not to undermine your confidence by criticising your accuracy. But two factors make you work at it – your own pride, and the fact that one day soon you will be in for yet another check-ride, and by then you had better be extremely accurate.

First, the normal circuit. Position at initials three miles out, at between 1,000 and 2,000 ft, and at 350 knots. You call initials and set 78 per cent rpm, then try to work out the effect that the wind will have. At this level in the Hawk, you have to compensate for the wind. The recommended figures for the circuit and the circuit pattern are all calculated for winds of 10–15 knots. If the winds are less or more you need to make adjustments, or you never will achieve the accuracy. If there is a crosswind component, nominate a downwind heading that will give you an accurate downwind leg without you being blown wide or tight, and tuck that heading figure away in your memory. You are approaching the airfield fast. Arrive deadside at 1,000 ft, look out for other aircraft, fly past the upwind end of the runway, select idle and airbrake, and turn downwind. Aim for 190 knots at the start of the downwind leg. Fly your nominated heading, check your height, make the RT downwind call, including your intentions, cram in the before-landing checks, trim, ease off the power to give 150–160 knots, watch the wingtip come into line with the threshold, tip in to your finals turn with 45 degrees angle of bank and 6 degrees nose down, select full flap, trim, select gear down, RT call finals with your intentions, either to roll or full stop, keep it coming round, aim to roll out at 200 to 300 ft and 130 knots, on a two-and-a-half degrees glideslope, remember the doughnut from your instructor of long ago, fly through it, point the nose at the threshold and adjust the throttle to give you the speed, keep it coming down, keep it coming down, keep it coming down, don't let the power come below 70 per cent, decide whether you like it or want to go around, this looks all right so we shall make it a roller, check three greens, full flap, and toes clear of the brakes, should be about 110 knots at the threshold, here we go, close the throttle to idle, press the stick back to bring the nose up, and there is a gentle thump as the main gear comes down. Excellent.

As this is a touch-and-go, keep the nosewheel up, steer with the rudder, apply full power, and off it flies at 110 knots. Look out for traffic downwind and joining the circuit, and in an instant you have 190 knots and it is time for the downwind turn.

It all happens at amazing, unnerving speed. You are busy, pressured, almost overwhelmed by the workload. And you have to do this over and over again. Sometimes it might be a low-level circuit, with your turns to downwind and from there to finals at only 500 ft. Sometimes it will be flapless, where you must go wider downwind, and remember to fly a shallower approach, with 150–160 knots as you roll out on short finals, and apply very little round-out.

Thankfully, just as you begin to tire and fear that your brain will reject all the knowledge it has, your instructor takes control and flies a perfect demonstration circuit. You sit back and watch him through it, and note where your own faults have been, so when you take control again it seems to get easier, and you begin to feel comfortable with your flying again. After the flight he goes through your faults – late round-out on one circuit, too early bringing back the throttle on another, which gave us a hard landing. But he approved of your lookout, which was good airmanship, and at this stage he tells you he is less worried about accuracy than about airmanship. Overall, things are going well.

Some people say that you can tell a fighter pilot from other pilots by the way he reacts to his first formation flight. Those who come down from the formation sortie with a gleam in their eye are going to make it. Those who are slightly green are not going to enjoy life in the fast-jet world. Formation flying is an important part of the advanced course. After the usual thorough and elaborate briefing, we walk to the aircraft and strap in. Our call sign is Taboo: Taboo One and Taboo Two. Formation flying might be either close formation, or tactical formation. The reason for learning to fly close formation is simple. Sending two aircraft up as a single unit saves time on the runway, and saves airspace. In war, it is essential that controllers are able to take off and land more than one aircraft at once. There is simply no time to handle them in the circuit separately. If they can be landed in groups of two, three, or even four aircraft, they can be turned round fast, and sent back into operation.

Line up on the runway. The leader, Taboo One, is on the left, in the centre of his half of the runway. We are in the centre of our

right-hand half of the runway, echeloned behind him. We operate
the standard procedure, with a system of hand signals, to convey
orders from the leader to our aircraft. Watch him carefully. He
rotates his forefinger, the universal signal to wind up the engines.
Holding the aircraft on the brakes, we advance the throttle to full
power, check the rpm and turbine gas temperature (TGT), and
drop the power by 2 per cent, then give the thumbs up that we
are ready. The leader lifts a white-gloved hand and taps his
helmet, once, twice, then nods his head vigorously forwards, and
simultaneously releases his brakes. The nod is a small moment of
drama, our signal to go, and we release the brakes at exactly that
moment. The Hawk is rolling, slowly at first, then with sudden
rapid acceleration, and the pair picks up runway speed to 95
knots. Then the leader's nosewheel lift off, and ours lifts, and at
100 knots his main gear lifts off and he is flying, and we are
following him, our heads angled hard left, and our eyes fixed on
the reference points.

The reference points depend on which cockpit seat the pilot
occupies. For the first lesson the student will be in the rear cockpit.
The aim is to place the leading edge of the wing fence of the
leader's aircraft in the angle between the UHF aerial and the
bottom of the fuselage. Then you position out just far enough to
look along the trailing edge of the tailplane. By a process of
triangulation, those points will place us in exactly the right position, at exactly the right distance away, and at exactly the right
spacing below the lead aircraft. With your head riveted to the left
you stare at those points. They are all that you have. Fly on them,
because your performance, your survival on the course, even your
life, depend upon it. Ideally, you should not have to use the throttle
much. The aircraft should perform like a matched pair, and only
the gentlest touches will keep you flying in the right position.
Everything depends on your flying attitude, and on your station-
keeping in pitch. If you climb you will fall back. If you descend
you will speed up. As you go round a turn with your aircraft on
the outside, you will have further to fly, so you need to open the
throttle, but only slightly. If you start round the inside of the turn
you need to close it slightly. It needs only the gentlest of touches,
and learning that kind of sensitivity is an important part of your
flying. Similarly the control stick. Only the slightest variations in
pressure are needed, to restore the picture as it starts to change.

The smaller the departure from the pattern, the less the need to fly back into it, and the more accurate the formation.

Eyes fixed on him, you are climbing smoothly away. You feel for the gear and flap buttons, and operate them without daring to look. You arrive at the cloud base and cloud comes swirling between the two aircraft, like thick impenetrable white messy fog. Fortunately it is never so thick that you lose sight of the lead aircraft, though in your early flights that was your worst fear. Then suddenly you burst out into the bright sunlight and blue sky overhead. In your peripheral vision you see the tops of the clouds fall away, shrugged off decisively behind you. But you dare not pause to admire the view – just stare resolutely at those reference points on the lead aircraft.

It is a long time since you flew formation in the Tucano. You have not got your hand in yet after five weeks in ground school, so your first attempt is decidedly rusty. As you take control, the lead aircraft suddenly changes its behaviour and drops towards the earth. You advance your stick to follow him down, and he seems to pull back on his and soar skywards. You are wrong, of course. He is flying smoothly straight and level, and it is your hamfistedness that is confounding your efforts. Try again. *Smoothly.* As your left and right hands come into some kind of co-ordination, the flying improves, and the two aircraft seem at least to be trying to maintain a consistent relationship. You begin to drift up in relation to the reference points. Lower the nose, just slightly, and ease back on the throttle a touch. Now you are flying back into place. Then you are going slightly low, so raise the nose, and you are slowing down, so adjust the throttle slightly to compensate. Small pressure adjustments are all that you need, provided you are quick to see the change in pattern.

To see again the standard expected, you ask the instructor to show you his work. In his hands, the Hawk sits glued to its position on the wing of the lead aircraft. Clearly the lead pilot and your instructor have a secret communication system. The other aircraft never seems to diverge from its steady flight path, and there is no apparent change in our relative position, or at least none big enough for you to perceive, before he has responded with a touch on the controls and kept the formation perfectly in harmony. Then you realise that you are not flying straight and level at all. The leader has turned to starboard, and is flying well above you.

Then he levels out and gradually turns to port, and your instructor follows, climbing high above the other aircraft, and you are convinced that you will soon fall down on to him. That doesn't happen. The two ships just proceed like a matched pair, putting on more and more bank and pulling more and more g. Students are expected to fly formation at up to 120 degrees of bank and 3 g, through a wingover.

You try it again yourself. This time, having seen again how precisely it can be done, you achieve a closer approximation to the ideal picture, dropping the nose just a touch as you go high on your reference points, and advancing or closing the throttle with a touch of pressure as he appears to be getting behind or ahead.

Throughout the formation flight, you have no idea where the leader is taking you. You simply continue to stare at the reference points on his aircraft and ignore everything else in the world. Only your peripheral vision tells you occasionally that the cloud layers are vertical, and you are carving through a huge banked turn. Keep your nerve. You are not going to fall out of the sky on to him. Both aircraft are behaving perfectly, and your success and safety depend on your smooth, confident flying, not on your separation from your formation partner. Even so, you know that you need a lot more practice, and you are grateful when he signals you, with a push of his opened palm against the side of the canopy, to relax the formation and pull away into your next phase, tactical formation.

Rarely, in modern operations, do aircraft work alone, and pilots need to learn to be part of a formation of two or more aircraft, as either the leader or wingman. Controlling other aircraft as well as your own, and knowing what is expected of you in response to control instructions, is learned through tactical formation flying. The basic tactical formation used in the Royal Air Force consists of a pair of aircraft flying in what is called defensive battle. The two aircraft fly at 2,000 yds separation in line abreast. At that separation the other aircraft looks distant, small, and solitary, and you feel somewhat solitary in your own Hawk. But the arrangement is effective. Each pilot can look out behind the other and check his six o'clock. Sometimes the patrol might consist of more than one pair, in which case they stack up behind each other, keeping a continuing lookout behind, and a large formation like that becomes virtually impenetrable, an almost invulnerable target for enemy aircraft. The disadvantage of a pair in defensive battle is that the formation is somewhat unwieldy. Any sort of turn would take the aircraft out of line abreast, unless the inside aircraft slowed abruptly. The task for the student is to learn to manoeuvre the formation, and to respond reliably to manoeuvring orders from the leader.

We are at medium level, 7,000 ft, high above the cloud tops. Out there on the starboard side the leader seems miles away. Remember the guidelines. If you can distinguish his canopy you are a bit tight. If he looks too small you might be a bit rangy. Adjust your range with a 10 degree turn towards or away. Even the experts find it difficult to judge. At 2,000 yds the other aircraft also seems to be slightly ahead of you, so be prepared for that. On the other hand if he looks too far ahead or behind, gain or lose 20 knots until the picture comes right. Nobody can tell you how to do it at this speed and height and range. You will just have to rely on accumulating experience.

Ready to manoeuvre? The leader calls: 'Taboo, 90 degrees, port.'

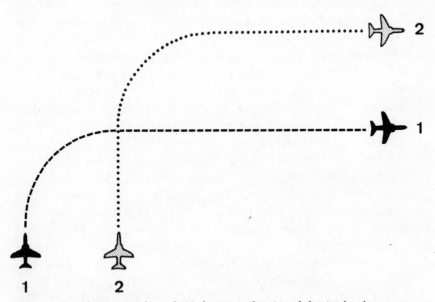

*Fig. 12* A simple tac turn through 90 degrees; pilots in a defensive battle formation need to fly the same distance and maintain the same speed, and to give each other support

He banks towards you from out on your starboard wing, and the familiar Hawk planform is silhouetted against the distant blue. Hold your position, hold it, then as he starts to move backwards along your canopy, bank into a 4 g turn yourself. You lose sight of him behind you. Look out over your left shoulder, and roll out of the turn on the 90 degree heading. He has come into view and is now flying out on your left wing (*see Fig. 12*).

'Taboo, 90 degrees, starboard.'

He banks towards you, becomes a planform silhouette, then drifts back along your canopy. Don't rush it, but turn now, 90 degrees to starboard, and there he is out on your starboard wing again. At times you will have to turn the formation through 180 degrees.

'Taboo, turnabout, starboard. Go.'

You bank and pull into a 4 g turn. This time you do not lose sight of him. If you keep a glancing eye on the direction indicator you should be in his six o'clock at precisely 90 degrees into the turn. Open or tighten the turn to make sure you hit the mark. Hold the g, and roll out in the 180 degree direction. Now he is away on your port wing, and you are both still protectively guarding each other's six o'clock. Keep a lookout.

'Taboo, turnabout, port. Go.'

And round you go again.

There are many other ways of turning the formation, with an Easy Turnabout, at 2 g; or the Tac 90, flown at 4 g; or the Double Assisted Turn, in which the two aircraft initially turn towards each other; or Variable Delay Turns; or the Rotate; or the Shackle. But those more complicated turns are not taught at this stage in the course. The pleasure is saved for later tactical training.

And break off for tailchasing. There are few more aesthetically satisfying flying experiences for the novice Hawk pilot than tailchasing. It is aptly named. Your task is to stay on the tail of the lead aircraft at a range of not less than 300 yds while he performs free manoeuvring in the sky. At 350 knots. Tailchasing feels like a great liberation from the confines of close formation or tactical formation flying. The leader is at liberty to fly any manoeuvres within a given height band. Your task is to fly in the same relative position. Tailchasing is an introduction to the expertise required for combat manoeuvring. If you cannot hold your position at 300 yds you will have difficulty staying on the tail of an opponent in a dogfight. It is best to start learning now.

The g is phenomenal. Your leader turns in great parabolas in the sky, with 96 per cent power set for the Adour engine. With uninhibited abandon, his aircraft sweeps majestically around the sky, in enormous turning manoeuvres – loops, rolls, barrel rolls, wingovers, as he tries, in theory at least, to shake you off his tail and throw you 'out'. If you get ahead of him you are out. If you fall too far behind you will be out. Your only hope is to keep him in the correct position in relation to your cockpit, and adjust your flight path if he threatens to put you at a disadvantage.

The technique is known as lead and lag. If he is getting too far away, so that you become 'stretched' you pull a margin more g and turn slightly inside him. Your smaller turning circle will enable you to catch up. If you are getting too close, you put on a margin of lag, aiming your turn slightly behind his to get more separation. As he reverses his turn, you follow him round, applying lead or lag as necessary. Lead and lag are also used to adjust your 'angle off', which is the angle between your 12/6 line and his. Lead will increase that angle. Lag will reduce it, and provided you can maintain the right range, can put you in a firing position in his six o'clock.

You glance at the altimeter. You are at 10,000 ft, and he is beginning to pull out of his dive. You pull up and follow him, going down as low as 7,000 ft before you begin to climb again. The Hawk has all the reserves of energy you need, and you climb out into a huge curving loop, pulling 5 g, until the aircraft seems to shake from the buffet caused by the airflow. Too much buffet. You remember what you learned about light buffet giving the best manoeuvrability. Relax the pull, and follow him round, keeping him in the angles formed by the pattern of the miniature detonating cord embedded in your canopy. You glance at the altimeter and see it reads 20,000 ft. You have gone up in an enormous climb, and now you are coming down the other side. He is getting too far away, so you pull to apply some lead. The g suiting is pumping against your legs and abdomen. You appear to be catching up, and he gets again to the end of his dive and starts to pull up, then banks into a wingover. You follow into the wingover, relaxing the g and putting on lag as he seems to grow bigger in the canopy. Now he is getting out of sight as he pulls up into the sun. Hold the turn, and follow him round, and he comes out of the sun and down the other side into a new dive.

For a minute or two you have lost all sense of where you are in the sky, as you let him lead you round in free manoeuvres, concentrating only on maintaining your relative position, and on not getting thrown 'out'. Meanwhile your canopy has cut the cloud horizon, out of the blue and into the white, and out of the white and into the blue, at every conceivable angle, and migrated between 7,000 and 20,000 ft more times than you could count.

You are learning something of the rudiments of air combat, at a simple level at this early stage, but this introduction will confirm whether you have the taste for that particular brand of liberated flying.

You also now have to learn how to transition to low level. Low-level flying is a hefty part of your training in the advanced stage of the course, but you will need to route to low-level flying areas with a high-level transit, to reduce fuel consumption and give you the increased range necessary.

At high level the air is thin, and the available thrust from the engine reduces. At 40,000 ft it is only a quarter of its sea-level value. The thrust available for climbing or manoeuvre is limited, and in the thin air, most of the control deflections produce little response. The aircraft has more momentum, and is less man-oeuvrable longitudinally. But because of its reduced aerodynamic damping, it has increased rolling manoeuvrability. The result is an aircraft that wallows, and is less controllable than down on the deck.

There are also some peculiar psychological effects. It is a feature-less landscape at 40,000 ft, with a great deal of glare. It becomes difficult to focus, and you need to be careful of your navigation. And since there are few external reference points, you have little sense of your speed, any more than you have in an airliner at 35,000 ft. It is only when you have a close reference point that you begin to feel the reality of high-speed flying. Most students find it a relief to descend from this unreal world, to a level where the aircraft behaves as you expect it to, and there are reference points against which you can gauge its performance.

The first reference point in the descent is the layer of cloud itself, on this winter's day a cotton wool infinity in every direction. But we need to find a way down through it, and the leader sets off on a high-speed search for a suitable hole. Swooping left and right like swallows at suppertime, we tear across the cloud peaks, searching over the canopy sides for a sight of the ground. The lead pilot seems to have an instinct for it. One brief view of the ground appears, and I expect him to turn back for it. He ignores it and flies on, putting in rapid 2 g turns, left, right, left, clearly enjoying flying among the cloud peaks. We have to match his turns, staying echeloned behind him on his 60 degree line as accurately as we can, where he can see us in his cockpit mirror.

A gap appears suddenly, larger than the first, and he starts to descend. The brilliant light above the cloud disappears, and is replaced by a uniform bleak greyness, with the brown hills beneath us. We have replaced the troughs and peaks and valleys of the cloud layer with real troughs and peaks and valleys in the ground below, and the leader romps off again for another hair-raising chase in fighting wing formation.

'Fighting wing is too close to be a usable tactical formation, but is used in bad weather, and in valley flying, where there is insufficient room for the separation of defensive battle. Ideally, the wingman should stay between 200 and 500 yds behind the leader, at a sweep angle of 60 degrees behind the line through his wings. If the range reduces towards 200 yds you cross to the outside of his turn.' It happens quite a lot as the leader climbs.

We are flying around the hills and valleys of North Wales. The ground is a random changing pattern of browns, dotted with grey stone buildings and white sheep, looking unconcerned at our arrival and instant departure. Time and time again the leader pulls 3 g and 4 g turns along the valleys and away from the hillsides. How he navigates at this speed and with these turns I have no idea, but I shall be expected to do it myself by the end of the course. 420 knots is 480 mph. We are cleared to 500 ft for this first sortie. Later we shall fly all our low-level navigation at 250 ft. Your barometric altimeter is no guide at these levels; it does not have the capacity to read the undulations in the ground. And the Hawk has no radio altimeter, which could do the job if only you had time to glance down and read it. Pilots have to rely on their judgement and experience to fly the altitude. They say you can count the legs on the sheep at 250 ft, and the legs on the cows at 500 ft. But the animals never stay in the same place for long enough to count anything at this speed, and you are concentrating too intently on the evolving picture ahead to look at the details.

Fighting wing is not a rigid formation, and the only firm rule is to stay above the leader, recovering the ideal sweep angle when we cross over, and using lead and lag to maintain the separation, turning and jinking, climbing and diving with the contours of the land.

The serious aim of this training is not merely to flush through the adrenalin glands, but to deliver bombs to targets without being shot down. The lower you are, the less chance the defences have to see you and shoot you down, so, once you have learned to fly at low level, you must train to navigate at low level. Low level is 250 ft. The speed is 420 knots. Throughout the air forces the speeds are worked in multiples of 60, so that calculation is simplified, and you can work out times and distances in your head, often in the course of a sortie.

The standard Bulldog speed was 120 knots – 2 nm per minute. In the Tucano it was 240 knots – 4 nm per minute. Now, in the Hawk, at 420 knots, you are travelling 7 nm in every minute. A typical training exercise at RAF Valley will involve a hi-lo-hi navigation route, with two or three initial point (IP)-to-target runs *en route*. That means a high-level transit to the low-level area, and similarly home. At two or three points *en route* you descend to low level, at a pre-planned point on the map, and fly to a target. You succeed if you can overfly the target accurately with wings level. Wales and most of Scotland are available for the exercise, and Hawk students have special CAA permission to fly down to 250 ft – half the minimum height allowed to private and commercial pilots in any area where they are likely to encounter people or buildings.

Navigating at these speeds and heights is challenging. Half the secret, as always, lies in the planning. We shall be flying over North Wales, and our target is a disused railway bridge over the River Dee. We are given the grid coordinates for the Ordnance Survey Map. Take out the map and study it.

Students on their final handling test, the culmination of the Hawk course, are given about 30 minutes to identify and plot their attack. They develop a facility which non-pilots, and even experienced non-military pilots who normally work at 2,000 ft and above, never need to develop. Non-military pilots get used to seeing the world in plan form, and interpret the map as a horizontal picture. From 2,000 ft the contours are not discernible, so you use railway lines, the patterns of woods, water, and roads to guide you. Down at 250 ft you can see few of those, but the contours are certainly visible, sometimes up round your ears, and you need to develop the technique of interpreting the map as a vertical picture just as you will see it developing ahead. You must read the pattern of contours from the map, and translate it into shapes of mountains and valleys. You must look for features that have a strong vertical component: a church may be hardly visible from above, tucked away among the trees, but its spire could be just the feature you need in flight at 250 ft. A wood might have a beautifully distinctive outline on the map, but further scrutiny shows that it lies on the far side of a slope, and you will not see it until you are right over it, so it is no use to you.

Fast-jet students develop the technique of tilting the map away from them, at least figuratively, and in the early stages even physically, to look for features that have a clear vertical dimension, and will be visible on a low-level sortie. Armed with this developing talent, you can study the map and decide on the best approach to your target. You start to look for a straight line to it, from any point of the compass, which has some distinctive features on it. Then you search for an IP. Ideally, the IP should be more than a minute but not more than two minutes from the target.

Using a ruler, we can work out a good clear run, up the valley of the Dee, overlying the end of Lake Bala, which makes a respectable check point. Combat pilots avoid overflying water. It makes them too visible from overhead. The route also gives us a good IP, the trig point at 337 m on top of a small distinctive hill. Draw the line between the IP and the target, but break the line to avoid drawing over any distinctive features on the track. Using the plastic template, mark off the 10 second points relating to 420 knots airspeed. Mark in also the distinctive points on the track, and estimate their times for overflying. The end of the wood on the hillside to the right of track should come up at 38 seconds, and the clearing on the edge of the wood by the road and river should come up at 58 seconds. After that, if we are on track and on time, we should reach the bridge at 1 minute 22 seconds. Calculate the magnetic heading, using the protractor and adding the variation for the area, and mark it in close to the IP, with a triangular arrowhead.

Write in the target, Bridge, as a reminder of what we are looking for on this run. Now study the map again, to identify any problems. There is, among other things, another railway bridge over the river, 12 seconds before the target; we shall have to remember that our target is the second bridge.

Now back to the Low Flying Chart, the LFC, to plan our approach to the IP. We select a start point in the area where our low flying is to take place, on the edge of a wood, close by a large lake.

Mark in the target, in its triangle, and the IP, with a square. Draw in a pre-IP, which is the turning point for the approach to the IP, on a heading which is close enough for a smooth turn. Draw in another turning point, this time the 863-ft hill outside Porthmadog, and link them up. The plastic has a circular hole, the circumference of which gives the radius of a 2 g turn at 420 knots in a Hawk, so you can draw a set of arcs with it, and link them with a clear line. Calculate the heading of each leg of the navex (navigation exercise), right back to your starting point, and write the heading in under an arrowhead. Mark in the minutes from the starting point, together with the exact times in minutes and seconds of each of the turning points. At the IP, where you will restart the watch, write in the elapsed times from the new zero. After the target, draw in a suitable escape heading, and mark the time of the finishing point for the exercise.

Now comes the really tricky part, folding the map. First the Ordnance Survey. Fold it lengthwise, parallel with the IP-to-target run, about 3 in. on each side of the track, with all your information visible; 6 in. to the outsides of those folds, tear along the length of the map. Refold it so that you have three layers. Fold it similarly 3 in. or so from the beginning and end of the run, and turn the ends under. Now you can take the fold to one side of the run, and tuck it neatly into the pocket you have formed with the ends and the other side. Smooth out all the creases with the edge of your ruler, and you have your target run clearly in front of you on a stiff piece of paper. Fold it in two to make it a suitable size, and you can hold it up like a card, flipping it at the half-way point in the run. It sounds complicated, but comes easily after a demonstration or two. You cannot afford to have large sheets of loose paper floating about in the cockpit at 420 knots, so fold your other target runs similarly, as well as your low-flying chart with the relevant area showing. Assemble them into a pile so that you can pull them out of your flying suit pocket in the right order, without risk of confusion.

We are approaching our start point. Set the throttle to give 420 knots and be ready to monitor the speed. Take out the low-flying chart. There is the wood, with the lake beyond it, so that is our start point. Map up in front of us. The heading is 249, so turn on to it. We have 3 minutes 25 seconds for the leg, so hack the watch, note the next major feature, and put the map down. Fly the heading. And look out. On a real run, we would be vulnerable to defending aircraft, so it is vital to keep a good lookout. Many a student has failed his test because he fixed his eyes in front of him and forgot about everything else.

We should be crossing the edge of a wood after one minute. Now comes the complication. Dead ahead of us, the countryside is obscured by a huge curtain of rain. Flying into that weather is suicide, so we have to think quickly what to do. At 7 mpm the student must be decisive, ready to change a plan, and continually have an idea about how to get back on plan. We swing right, into a clearer patch. Now the plan has gone completely awry. We make our way to the north, turning with the contours again, looking ahead for a possible left turn. We have turned back on to the parallel track, and out there to the left an orange glow is visible behind the rain. It is a clear patch of sunlight, and it must be close to our track. We dive down into it, and find ourselves out of the mountains and on to the coastal plain, with Porthmadog five miles ahead.

It takes confidence to diverge from the track, turn back on to it, and know that you are going to pick up the plan again, even if a minute or so late. But my instructor has a philosophy that encourages that kind of confidence: 'Even if you turn away at right angles and fly for a full minute you are only going to be seven miles off track. By then you should have found a way round the weather and you can fly back for a minute. Changing your track doesn't mean you are lost. It just means you have to rethink your plan.'

We fly between a pair of villages, so as not to disturb the inhabitants, and pull the Hawk round the outside of the 863-ft hill, then bank further and pull more g to keep north of the coast and outside the danger area.

Check the time, 20 seconds late, and turn on to the new heading, 109 degrees. Map away again, and we are looking for a road along a valley where it disappears into a wood. It would have been at 5 minutes 15 seconds. We shall expect it at 5 minutes 35 seconds. And our next heading will be 080 degrees; 5 minutes 20 coming up, there is the wood ahead, and we turn now. Everything is happening with astonishing speed, and we are looking for the next wood, with the hill in the clearing. Target map out of pocket now, and hold it up with the left hand in front of us. Check speed, and at 6 minutes 30 seconds we can see the wood ahead, with that small hill at the centre. Ready to turn on to 078 degrees and hack the watch, now.

A long run across the end of Lake Bala, and look for that wood on the hillside. We are too far to the right, so *wham*, roll the Hawk left, pull, roll back right, pull, and we have left the wood on our right and are back on the 078 degrees heading.

Flip the map over, and expect to see the next wood, the one with that bite out of it, coming up on the nose at 58 seconds. There is the wood and the river goes off to the right. The disused railway is just down to the left, and there is the first bridge, which we do not want, and on the nose the second bridge . . . ah it is missing. Just a couple of pontoons left standing in the water. But we overflew the target with wings level.

Bank to the right before we leave the valley and on to our escape heading of 203 degrees. Put the target map away. Relax slightly, and look out; 3 minutes 20 seconds coming up, and there is the lake ahead, and the end of the exercise. We take a minute for a breather and climb round the southern edge of the lake, admiring the fairy-tale castle out on the end of the causeway.

For the early student, everything in the course of that low level navigation route, and especially in the course of the run to the target, happens at breakneck speed, and it seems impossible to take anything in. But having built up to it, through the Bulldog course, and certainly at 240 knots during basic training on the Tucano, the able Hawk pilot at the end of this course will have no real difficulty in flying his route accurately, diverting and regaining the route if he has to, and putting in an accurate run to the target. Watch, map, ground . . . watch, map, ground. The process is logical, and with practice becomes less demanding. But it never gets any less exciting, however many target runs you fly.

On your final handling tests, you have to demonstrate that you can do all this, and a great deal more. You will certainly be asked to demonstrate your ability to cope with emergencies.

'Abort for bad weather.' We have to gain height at the best possible angle, to avoid possible high ground ahead, so throttle fully forward, pull 4 g into the climb, and hold the nose up at 30 degrees. Keep the wings level using the attitude indicator, and . . . *whoosh*, we are out of the clouds and back into the sunlight at 7,000 ft.

'And if you would like to show me your aerobatics sequence.'

Each of the three squadrons at 4 AFTS has its own aerobatics list, which the student is expected to master and be able to demonstrate in a continuous flowing sequence, and to an accurate line. There are minor variations on what you have learned at the elementary and basic levels. For instance, the Hawk does not like a stall turn, since it disturbs the intake airflow and risks an engine surge.

You are straight and level at 350 knots and 7,000 ft. If you can see the ground pick a line feature, or if you are above cloud choose a distinctive formation. If neither of those is possible, note your heading so that you can fly back on to it after a manoeuvre. Also nominate your base height, say 10,000 ft, and a gate height, say 17,000 ft, which will be your apex height for vertical manoeuvres. Fly up to it, and you know you can pull out safely from that height as you descend.

Start with a loop. Select full power and fly along the line at your base height at 330 knots. Pull up into a 4 g climb, and hold the wings level. You can feel the g-suit inflate, and it reminds you to tense up your muscles – stomach, chest, and arms, especially your arms – as you need to keep absolute control of the stick and throttle. As you go towards the apex of the loop, relax the g slightly to keep it on that light buffet, and pull over the top. As you gain speed down the other side, look up through the top of the canopy and watch for the horizon, and keep the wings level. Monitor the height and pull more g or relax it to bring you smoothly back on to 7,000 ft.

Straight into your next manoeuvre, the half horizontal eight. At 330 knots pull up with 4 g. It is just like the entry to the loop.

Look up for the horizon, and as you go over the top reduce the power to 90 per cent. Keep the aircraft coming down the other side. Don't rush it. Wait until you are gaining speed, and check the attitude indicator to watch for the nose coming to 60 degrees nose down. There it is, so transfer to the altimeter, and at 14,000 ft put the stick hard over to roll the aircraft upright, centralise the stick, and ease out of the dive at your base height, on the reciprocal of your entry heading.

And into a four-point roll. Let's roll to the right, since everybody tends to go to the left. Look out, and set 90 degrees rpm. Roll the aircraft to the right through 90 degrees, and apply a good bootful of left rudder to keep the nose up. Hold it counting, one, and two . . . and roll right to inverted, centralise the rudder and ease the stick well forward to keep the nose from coming down. Hold it, one, and two . . . and roll right again to wings vertical and apply a lot of right rudder. Ease the stick back, and hold it, one, and two . . . and roll it to the right again, centralising the rudder as we come upright. You hear the hiss of your own breath in your headset. Difficult, that one: very hard to fly accurately.

Now straight into a maximum rate turn. Take a good lookout. Entry speed 300 knots. Full power, roll on the bank and smoothly pull 6 g to the buffet. Keep the nose on the horizon and smoothly ease off the g, then roll out of the turn after 180 degrees.

And into your barrel roll, with a good lookout, full power, speed up to 330 knots, pull 4 g to bring the nose up to 60 degrees, roll the aircraft and keep pulling, keeping the pitch and roll going, and you should ease out of the roll at base height. It is different from the diving barrel rolls you learned, but you are handling a high-speed jet now, so be confident; show you have mastered it. Into your next manoeuvre. Start it with a max rate turn again, hard through 180 degrees, then through 45 degrees more until you are oblique to your start line. Now for the manoeuvre itself, the Derry turn. Check forward gently on the stick, to ease off the g, and roll under with aileron until you have 60 degrees of bank in the other direction, and pull to the line. That one is quite disorienting.

Ready for your half Cuban eight. Entry at 330 knots, full power, pull up at 4 g, and 60 degrees nose up again. Check wings level and at 2,000 ft above base height roll inverted, and as you approach your gate height pull through, reduce the power to 90 per cent as you go through the top of the manoeuvre, and pull through the second half just as for the loop. Ease it out, more g, more muscle, and there she comes on 10,000 ft.

Are we going on with this demonstration, you wonder briefly? Is your examiner letting you continue because he is full of admiration, or because he is waiting to see if you can get one of them right before he asks you to give up. There are no indications from the rear seat, so into the slow roll, which is a smoothly flowing version of the four-point roll you managed earlier, and on to a max rate turn to the right, through 270 degrees, to face your line. Think of it as the crowd at a flying display. Next, the quarter clover leaf. Before you arrive at the line select full power. You will need more momentum for this manoeuvre, so let the speed build up to 350 knots, then pull hard up with the familiar 4 g. Keep the wings level and ease off the pull as you go into the vertical. Look along the wing for a clear feature and roll gently towards it. Now look over your head to put that feature in the centre of the canopy, then pull through towards it. Throttle back to 90 per cent rpm, and continue the pull, easing out of the dive 2,000 ft above base height to level off at 10,000 ft.

And we are still going on, so let's do the vertical roll. We need even more energy for this, so full power and up to 370 knots, and a good pull to 5 g. Wings level, and on to light buffet. Ease off the buffet as we fly to the vertical. Select a feature off the wing, and start a roll through 360 degrees back to the feature. Keep the aircraft flying vertically through that, and now ease the stick back to pull through, set idle power when inverted. Hold it until you are nose down directly towards the ground. Pick a feature off the wing and roll through 360 again, back to the feature. And start to pull out, 3,000 ft above base height. Then power on and fly out level at 10,000 ft.

'That's the end of my sequence, sir.'

'OK, then take us back to base for a radar recovery, and a flapless circuit and full stop.'

In the crew room, afterwards, the atmosphere resembles a good funeral. Most of the course are elated. They have taken their final handling tests and all have passed. There is only one student left. The squadron grapevine is working at high speed. Almost before he has come in for his debriefing, the rumour is around that there are problems. The only hope is that he can go back and use some of his available flexible time and retake the test. He is undergoing his debriefing now.

His is the body at the funeral, the reminder of mortality, the one blot on a clean sheet that would generate universal celebration. He is the outsider. The others are sympathetic, but they have passed. Somehow the message gets around before he is even out of the door. A hand across the throat signals somebody's certain knowledge that he has not made it. Chopped.

There is no appeal. No second chance. The CFI has spoken, and that is the end of it. An inadequate performance in any aspect of the test can indicate an inability to cope with the fast-jet environment. And if the CFI, even at the end of the course, has doubts about what he sees, he will – must – chop the student. It was the close-formation flying that gave him doubts this time. The student fell behind on take-off and failed to get the power on fast enough to recover his position. He completed the test, parts of it perfectly well, but that one fault in his flying was enough to banish him permanently from fast jets.

It is a tough, brutal world. But the CFI has the student's safety, and the safety of those who would ultimately have been flying alongside him, possibly in a war, to consider.

The chopped student has two main options. He can go to transport flying or rotary wing. He opts for re-streaming on the rotary wing course, where he will learn to fly helicopters. Things happen at lower speeds there, but nobody will tell you it is easier than fast jets. In command of a helicopter, at night in foul weather, searching for a downed pilot off the Scottish coast, can require courage and flying aptitude of a high order. It is not the same as fast jets, but it is no less demanding.

Nevertheless he will regard it, temporarily at least, as a failure, perhaps a humiliation, and his main task now is to learn to live with himself, and to find a way to stay cheerful among his friends for the last few hours of his course.

A couple of beers in the mess afterwards helps considerably. Cheerfulness returns, and the CFI and the failed student are cordial together. The CFI might be thought heartless in his lack of regret at having to curtail such ambition; the student has come to terms commendably quickly with this sudden late career block. The reason for their mutual cheerfulness can be found in the CFI's explanation, in a view he shares with examiners at every stage of training: 'I have never known a chopped student yet who was not expecting it, and who was not mightily relieved when it finally came.'

The others have all passed, and will join the graduates of the course preceding theirs for a passing-out ceremony, at which they will receive their wings. Then they are off on leave before their next assignments. One of them, the most successful student on the course, has been creamed off and will go to the Central Flying School to learn to be an instructor himself. He is a 'creamie'. This is almost a new version of 'the few', the élite who are taken straight out of training to instruct other students of their own age, for at least one tour. Some 'creamies' are uncertain of the value of this accolade, and would rather have continued in training and gone on to a front-line squadron, which is what they joined the Royal Air Force for in the first place. But in this service their job is to go where they are told. Weapons training and operational flying will have to wait. The others are all going to do that. They are posted to a Tactical Weapons Unit (TWU) at either RAF Brawdy or RAF Chivenor where they will study how to combine proficiency in piloting a fast jet with acquiring skill as a highly sophisticated aerial marksman. It is a course which makes daunting demands on the commitment and ability of the students, but it is the gateway to operational flying and the newcomers are eager to start.

# 8

# Learning to Fight

The atmosphere at the TWU is quite different from that at the flying schools you have attended so far. The student/instructor relationship – until now a matter of distinctly different levels of status – undergoes a subtle change. Trainee pilots at the TWU are no longer merely students; they are full members of their squadrons. For the first time, pilots in training and their instructors share the same crew room, the same sandwiches and snacks, the same interminable brews of tea and coffee. Frequently they hold the same rank, and it can happen that trainees outrank their instructors. Nobody forces a student to fly. If he does not want to learn, nobody will push him or pressure him. There is a relaxed banter around the crew room, mess, and pubs that would seem out of place in the earliest stages of the student's training. It is an acknowledgement that you have arrived in the realm of the professional, where trainee and instructor alike are sharing a learning process, developing together the skill of the combat pilot.

The course introduction sums up the challenge: 'Your progress will reflect your determination to succeed, your own efforts, and your ability to be both self-critical and aggressive. This is not a course for the faint-hearted; if that is your disposition, or if you really don't want to become a fighter pilot, quit now. Otherwise, pick up the gauntlet.'

There are three main strands of learning in the tactical weapons course.

The first is a mixture of the familiar and the unknown. The aircraft used, the Hawk, is by now an old friend. What is unfamiliar is the device with which it has been equipped, a weapons sight for gunnery and bombing. The task now facing the student is that, in addition to piloting a fast jet, he must become adept at using it as

146

a moving platform from which to launch an attack on a specified target and score a dead hit.

The second element, designed to enable him to carry out attacks successfully, is air combat manoeuvring, and the purpose of the tactical weapons course is to introduce him to the exceptional handling-skills required. This initiation, both exacting and exciting, gives him the sound foundation on which he can build during operational conversion and as a junior pilot on his squadron. Most pilots enjoy this phase, and a lot of conversation at the TWU is illustrated with hands twisting in anatomically impossible directions – 'flying the wristwatch'.

The third and probably most important phase involves learning to operate the aircraft in the low-level environment, as part of a formation. The trainee will gain experience as both leader and wingman. Low-level attack flying is learned in a series of sorties known as Simulated Attack Profiles (SAPs). An SAP involves flying a route to a target, and carrying out a gun or bomb attack on it. It is an extension of the low-level navigation training at the Advanced Flying School. But it is set against a realistic intelligence scenario, and it always involves more than one aircraft. The student, acting as leader, must plan the route to two separate targets, plan the attacks against them having selected the appropriate weapons, and plan the return to base. He must brief and debrief the sortie, and he must control the formation throughout the flight.

In later SAPs, the route will be made known to two of the course instructors, also in Hawks, who will try to bounce the student's formation at points along the route. If the student can lead a formation from take-off to a bomb or gun attack on the range, score a dead hit, fly an accurate SAP, including two IP-to-target runs, keep a good-enough lookout to tally two aircraft trying to bounce his formation, and prevent them ever getting into a weapons-release position on him, he will be considered suitable to go on to the most demanding of front-line aircraft squadrons.

First, he must learn to use the weapons sight. Dropping bombs accurately, as taught at the TWU, is not precisely representative of the kind of weapons delivery that the young pilot will ever carry out on a squadron. The technique is not designed to teach him to operate modern front-line aircraft, but to form a practical introduction to a complicated topic. Weapons delivery in the modern fighter is integrated with the electronic navigation systems, and aided by head-up-display technology. At Chivenor the technology is more rudimentary, though complicated enough. There is another difference. Bomb delivery is taught here as a 10 degree dive-bombing exercise, which would leave the aircraft far too vulnerable on today's battlefield. In real life bombing is usually carried out from a level run.

Nevertheless, it is a sound teaching system, and puts demands on the student that will test his ability to perform at a high work level.

The weapons sight is a gyro-based instrument in which the aiming details are shown as a picture on a clear plate in front of the pilot's eye. The main picture for bomb aiming is a circular sight, with vertical lines and horizontal lines inside the circle, and horizontal lines and dots outside it. There is also a dot in the centre of the circle: the pipper (see Fig. 13).

The most important feature to remember about the sight is that the horizontal lines, and the gaps between them, subtend angles of 10 mils each. Fighter pilots use millage as the basis of their aiming. A mil is a milliradian, a thousandth part of a radian. It is a measure of an angle, as seen from the target.

The aim in bombing is to fly an accurate flight path over the

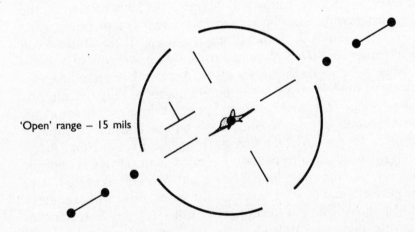

'Open' range – 15 mils

*Fig. 13* The view through the Hawk gunsight at the start of the ciné-tow

target. The pilot sets up the sight at a distance of 5,000 ft, or 1,667 yds. The sight then passes over the target, and the pilot 'pickles' the bomb. It should give him a DH, or dead hit.

As you approach the target, it will appear to grow in relation to the bomb sight. If you know the size of the target, you will know, by simple trigonometry, when you have reached a range of 1,667 yds. But it is essential to know the exact dimensions of the target. At the ranges used by the two TWUs, the bomb target is a circular patch of pale ground in an otherwise featureless expanse of Welsh coastal landscape. Its diameter is known, and at 1,667 yds it subtends precisely 30 mils in the bombing sight. All you have to do is wait until the target spreads to fill 10 mils for the gaps on each side of the pipper, and each half of the 10 mil lines to either side, and you can open, or 'uncage' the sight (*see Fig. 14*).

The Hawk control stick has a flap covering the bomb-release button. When you flick it with your right thumb, you uncage the sight, and also start the ciné-camera running, so that your performance can be assessed. Opening the flap causes the circular sight to fall away directly down the sight. Then you are left with two other small symbols; the important one at this stage is the Flight Path Bug, or FPB, a dot with a short line through it. Having set up the bombing pass, and uncaged the sight so that it falls

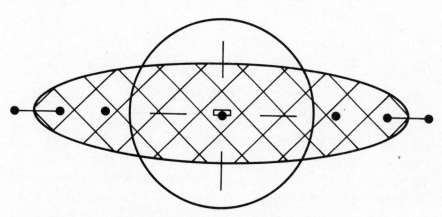

*Fig. 14* The view through the bomb-aiming sight at the target on the Pembrey range; the dots are 10 mils (milliradians) apart. Here, at 515 ft, the target subtends 97 mils – the 'pickle' picture in still air at standard temperature and pressure

away into the six o'clock position, you now have to maintain the same flight path. Do it by keeping the FPB in the same position on the ground that it occupied in the uncage position, then you will continue down the 10 degree flight path.

Finally, as you approach the release point, the sight begins to track forwards along the ground from its six o'clock position towards the target. There is a temptation here to try to fly the aircraft down to meet the sight. You avoid it by locking your arms to maintain the same flight path. That also leaves you free to take your eye off the FPB and concentrate on the sight. If you are flying the correct azimuth (direction across the ground) the sight will track directly up to the target and start to move through it. The pipper itself will pass through the centre of the target. As it does so, pickle the bomb.

In practice there is usually a small delay in the student's reaction, so he is advised to anticipate the bomb release slightly.

As the instructors summarise it: 'Sight over target; 30 mils; uncage; bug, bug, bug; lock your arms; pipper on target; pickle.'

That, in short, is the bomb-aiming system for still air at standard temperature and pressure. Air is rarely still, and its temperature and pressure are variable, so the pilot must adjust the sighting system to take into account the best available information on how wind, temperature, and pressure will affect the fall of his bomb.

First, the wind allowance. If an aircraft flies down a flight path at a set airspeed into a stiff headwind, it will fly at a steeper slope than in still air. The sight, therefore, has to be raised, and the rule is to raise the sight by 1.5 mils for each 10 knots of headwind. Lower it by 1.5 mils for every 10 knots of tailwind. Any crosswind will also cause the aircraft to bomb inaccurately, and you need to fly the aircraft down the path with its nose pointing into wind, so that it stays on track. A fixed reference point in the sight, in the form of an inverted T, shows where the aircraft is pointing, and for every 10 knots of crosswind you have to point the aircraft 25 mils into wind. This adjustment is achieved by dialling the crosswind component into the bomb sight on the way to the target.

Even with this aid, accounting for the wind in the course of an approach to a bomb run is a complicated activity and requires considerable mental gymnastics, once the bombing range officers have reported the wind velocity. You can now see the value of all that work you did in your early navigation course. It might not be of any value in navigation at the speeds of the fast jet, but the calculations are similar, and you have to be able to do them if you are going to drop bombs successfully on the TWU ranges. Your bomb-aiming calculation depends on understanding the simple sine rule. First, you work out the angle between your intended flight path and the wind direction. If the wind is on the nose it has a headwind component of 100 per cent. If it is from 90 degrees on either side you do not count it, as there is no headwind component. If the wind angle is 30 degrees you count half of it. If it is 60 degrees off you count all of it.

The sequence has to be followed carefully and rapidly. Remember the headwind component; raise the sight by 1.5 mils for every 10 knots, or lower it by 1.5 mils for every 10 knots of tailwind. Now remember the crosswind. Calculate it from the wind velocity, and dial in 25 mils for every 10 knots of crosswind component. Commit to memory the picture at the uncage range. Fly the FPB, and the vertical lines in the sight should track steadily up towards the target.

There is a second variable to take into consideration – the air density. An object travelling through the atmosphere will go faster or slower depending on the density of the air. Hot air is less dense than cold air, while air at lower atmospheric pressure is also less dense than air at higher pressure. For a given indicated airspeed, an aircraft will move more slowly over the ground in cold air at higher atmospheric pressure, than on a relatively hotter day at lower atmospheric pressure. The bomb sight must therefore be adjusted so that the bomb falls on target in the prevailing atmospheric conditions. That is achieved by calculating the depression. As a reference point the sight is set to a basic depression, which is 109 mils in international standard temperature and pressure conditions, for a typically loaded aircraft weight at the start of a sortie. The sight depression must be decreased by 1.5 mils for every 10°C of temperature increase (the aircraft will be flying faster, and so would otherwise tend to drop the bomb beyond the target). And the depression must be increased by 0.5 mils for every 10 mb of pressure increase, over the standard ICAN conditions.

There is less complication involved in this activity than seems likely, because the pilot can read off the required depression, for the temperature and pressure predicted at the target, on the graph in the sortie preparation room.

Having dropped the bomb at the end of a 400-knot dive, the pilot must pull up in a 5 g climb, to avoid flying straight into the ground. At the Pembrey ranges he then rolls into a 60-degree banked turn to keep out of the local danger area and come round for another pass.

Inevitably, it all seems formidably complicated to the new pilot, but, as with all other skills that have to be acquired before he can fly fast jets in combat, weaponry is learned item by item, and students are given plenty of practice. It is demanding, and a few find that they do not have the capacity to master these skills. But, for those who do, the build-up is rapid, and they are soon able to bomb accurately and with confidence, and to carry out strafing runs to the same level of accuracy.

If weapons operation requires a mixture of determination, precision, and unflappability, air combat calls for the skills of an aerial ballerina, the fighting instincts of a mongoose, and the logical responses of a chess grandmaster.

If he is serving with an operational squadron, the pilot must expect to be involved at some time in air combat. If he is employed in the air defence environment, he will probably fly supersonic fighters equipped with beyond-visual-range missiles, and will fly with the help of a navigator in the rear cockpit. Even so, when the enemy approaches, he will not be able to avoid closer contact with surviving aircraft, and will have to rely on his close manoeuvring skills and the agility of his aircraft to survive and defeat his enemy. If he is operating in the ground attack role, and succeeds in reaching his target and eliminating it, he will still have to return to base across hostile territory, and must expect defending aircraft to engage him. To survive these attacks, a pilot has to have a knowledge of the performance of his aircraft, especially of its turning rates, and a thorough familiarity with the weapons systems. He must also have a detailed knowledge of the performance of all the enemy aircraft he is likely to encounter, so that he can judge where to gain the advantage and where he might lose it. And, when he has learned the basic manoeuvres of air combat, he must know how to practise them in a pairs formation, so that he can fight effectively alongside his partner.

Nobody claims that all this can be taught or learned at the

TWU. In its trainer configuration, the Hawk is a limited aircraft in many respects – simple, subsonic, daylight only, with no radar and only a cannon for air-to-air combat. But it is agile and small, and has an excellent turn rate at low and medium altitudes and high speeds. Provided the indicated airspeed is above 400 knots, it will keep turning well at the light buffet, although the turn rate falls off if the speed falls below 350 knots, and at 300 knots reduces drastically. The engine also loses power rapidly as the altitude increases, so the best means of operating the Hawk in combat is to stay at relatively low levels, keeping the speed up at around 400 knots, and pulling to 'nibble' at the light buffet. It is an ideal aircraft for TWU students to learn and practise the basic air combat manoeuvres.

The aim in air combat manoeuvring is simple. If you are on the offensive, you manoeuvre to gain a position from which you can destroy an enemy. Assuming you are on the defensive, your sole aim is to prevent the enemy aircraft from gaining a position where he can release his weapons and hit you.

The weapons-release position on the Hawk is within 800 yds and 30 degrees angle-off for a gun, and within 2,000 yds and 120 degrees angle-off for a missile release at low level. These are only training guidelines. TWU students are warned that missiles work at longer ranges and greater degrees of angle-off at higher altitudes, and that missile performance is constantly being improved.

Air combat manoeuvring is filmed, for later analysis during the debrief, and the rules for claiming a kill in training are laid down according to what can be shown on the film. A pilot who can align his pipper within a pipper's width of the back of the other aircraft's cockpit for half a second, or eight frames of film, at ranges between 300 and 500 yds, has a training kill. If he can hold the pipper on any part of the aircraft at the same ranges for 2 seconds (32 frames) he also has a training kill.

Air combat has to start somewhere, and is set up by means of visual splits. With two aircraft flying in defensive battle formation, the leader can call, 'Outwards turn for combat. Go.' Both aircraft turn away through 45 degrees, maintaining visual contact. At the call, 'Inwards turn. Go', they turn towards each other through 135 degrees, to approach head-on. Air combat starts at the inwards turn, unless the leader elects to delay it until the crossover. An alternative start is for the leader to call, '270 outwards turn for combat. Go.' Sixty degrees of bank will turn the aircraft rapidly away from each other, and they roll out of the turn approaching head-on. Combat starts there.

There is almost no way to describe the joy to a pilot of air combat manoeuvring (ACM), at least in peacetime training. If he enjoyed learning aerobatics, he will find air combat irresistible. It is an extension of the aerobatics skills into a new, freer dimension. The formal patterns of aerobatics are abandoned, or at least modified, and there is the added excitement of a competing aircraft flying in close attendance. Together, these two aircraft leap and soar in three-dimensional space, turning, jinking, twisting, pulling g, ascending and descending, almost without limit. It can be tiring, and it can stress the aircraft, but if a pilot is an enthusiast for ACM, he is a real enthusiast, and one hand will be seen pointing at the other in conversations throughout the crew rooms, briefing rooms, and messes, and those who win tend to come back with satisfied grins.

Considerable advantage in basic ACM can be gained by employing g to good effect. It is illustrated in the air combat egg (*see* Fig. 15). As two opposing aircraft fly around in the horizontal plane in a 4 g turn, they will stay on opposite sides of the circle,

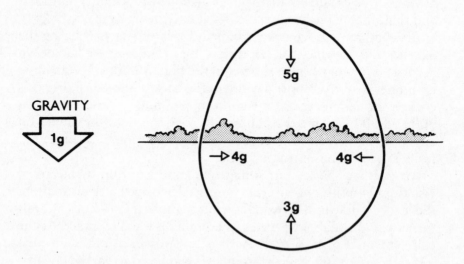

*Fig. 15* The combat egg, showing how gravity assists or opposes a loop, affecting the speed and turn radius

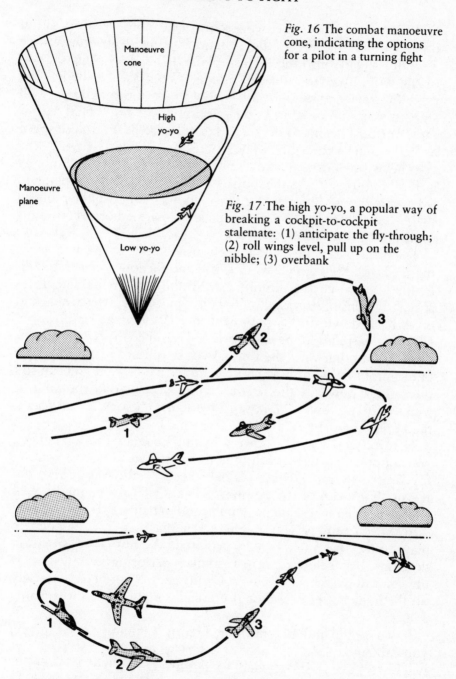

Fig. 16 The combat manoeuvre cone, indicating the options for a pilot in a turning fight

Manoeuvre cone

High yo-yo

Manoeuvre plane

Low yo-yo

Fig. 17 The high yo-yo, a popular way of breaking a cockpit-to-cockpit stalemate: (1) anticipate the fly-through; (2) roll wings level, pull up on the nibble; (3) overbank

Fig. 18 Its close relative, the low yo-yo; (1) overbank; (2) unload and accelerate; (3) gently ease back up to defender's level

and it is unlikely that either will get into a weapons-release position on the other. However, the situation changes as soon as one aircraft converts into the vertical plane, flying a loop. At the top of the loop, inverted, and still pulling a nominal 4 g, he has the force of gravity to aid him; he is now in a 5 g turn. Gravity will start to help him as soon as he goes above the horizontal, so his radius of turn begins to decrease. He will also begin to lose speed as he goes into the climb. The opposite is similarly true. As he goes below the horizon, and begins to pull back into the climb, he is fighting gravity. At the bottom of the turn, he is having to overcome the entire force of gravity, so his total g will be reduced by one, to 3 g. He will increase speed below the horizon, and his radius of turn will also increase.

The principle of the combat egg is used in two of the most basic manoeuvres: the high yo-yo (*Fig. 17*) and the low yo-yo (*Fig. 18*). In the high yo-yo the aircraft climbs above his opponent, loses speed, tightens his turn, pulls 4 g and achieves 5 g, overbanks, and dives back down on his opponent in an advantageous position. He will have reduced the angle-off, and regained the energy advantage. An alternative is the low yo-yo. If you are flying in a turn but cannot raise your nose sufficiently for a gun shot, you can roll the aircraft towards the inside of the turn, unload the aircraft (reduce the g), lower the nose to fly across the circle, and regain the horizontal plane.

Naturally, when you start yo-yoing to gain the advantage, your opponent will not continue to fly in a steady circle waiting for you to fly into his six o'clock. He will also start to yo-yo. If you both choose to go into a high yo-yo you might well end in a cockpit-to-cockpit climb, and stalemate. If you choose different directions you might arrive back in the manoeuvre plane with the advantage neutralised. As any such situation develops between aircraft of similar performance, then it is the aircraft which is flown smoothly and accurately, generally on the light buffet, which will gradually accumulate the advantage.

If you should find that the other aircraft is gaining the advantage, you can embark on a variety of defensive manoeuvres. Your aim will be to force your opponent to 'fly-through' or pass you in such a way that he cannot regain the weapons-release position behind you. The most effective defensive manoeuvre depends on sighting the attacker early, which is why from a very early stage in training the pilot is urged to maintain a good lookout. If you see your opponent early enough, you can simply turn towards him, and his chance of gaining the weapons-release position is negated. You then have a clear choice between making a head-on pass, and continuing with your sortie, or turning on him to initiate an offensive manoeuvre.

If all else fails, and your attacker is gaining the advantage in terms of position and energy, you can try a high g barrel roll. The technique is to close the throttle, reducing your speed to about 300 knots, and as your attacker begins to close, fly a tight, nose-high barrel roll. You should arrive in your attacker's six o'clock, but you will have reduced your energy drastically, and unless you can gain an immediate threatening position, you will need to disengage and set up another attack.

What will probably happen, should you manage to force your attacker to fly through, is that he will slow his aircraft to prevent you falling in astern of him. You will probably then find that you are flying in line abreast, and stalemate. Your best course is to start a maximum-rate turn towards him. His best course is to do precisely the same towards you, and you begin to cross and recross each other in a scissoring fight. The aircraft which makes the least forward progress will win, but you have to be careful not to stall. The aircraft which begins to gain the advantage can start to turn just before the other aircraft crosses his twelve o'clock, and start to move behind. If it is not you, your best bet is to plan to run out as the other aircraft crosses your nose, putting distance between you so that you are 2,000–3,000 yds away before he can complete his turn, and outside the weapons release envelope. Even so, you still have to be wary of a missile shot which can cover these ranges if the other aircraft is suitably equipped.

If your opponent chooses to fly a high yo-yo against you, you have a further option in responding. You can pull into a barrel roll up under him, and you will probably force him to fly through and separate. His next choice is to start a barrel roll of his own, and you will find that both aircraft start to fly a series of concentric barrel rolls. As you try to keep the other aircraft in your canopy, you can begin to judge whether you are gaining the advantage. If you are gaining the advantage he will appear to move forward in your canopy. If you are losing he will appear to be moving back along it. The winner will be the pilot who flies his aircraft to the best effect, maintaining his speed and turning on the light buffet. Too much g, and you will lose energy. Too little, and you will make excessive forward progress, so that he can fall in behind you. The only solution then is to wait until he is nose high and his speed is reducing, and disengage. Then you will find yourself descending at a fast rate, and you must take care not to fly through the base height.

All these manoeuvres have assumed that you are engaged in one-against-one combat. That is not inevitable, and part of training will be one-against-two, sometimes with you alone, sometimes with you leading the pair.

Offensive two-against-one combat is aimed at developing your aggressive combat attitude, developing your formation control, and teaching you to communicate effectively with your partner. One aircraft is engaged, fighting the bogey on a one-against-one basis, while the second aircraft gains energy and takes up an advantageous position.

You are beginning to learn the language of air combat. 'Bandit' is an unidentified and possibly hostile aircraft. 'Bogey' is a definitely hostile aircraft. 'Tally' means that you have the bandit in sight; 'visual' that you have your partner in sight. You might be 'engaged' (fighting the bogey) or 'free' (positioning for an attack) in which case when you return to the fight you will be 'engaging'. The bogey might be 'on you' or 'off you', or might have 'switched' from one aircraft to another, perhaps leaving you with your 'tail clear', and no bogey in your rear sector. You might have to 'counter' with a hard turn on the light buffet, or 'break' with a maximum-rate turn, to avoid a threat. Or a simple 'tac turn' might be called for, with 4 g and your speed maintained.

Fighting in a partnership of this kind, you clearly have duties and responsibilities. If you are free, your job is to gain separation from the fight, maintain tally and visual, gain as much energy as you need, and position to re-enter the fight with the advantage to achieve a quick kill. And you must keep your engaged partner informed of the combat situation, and make sure that both your own and his six o'clock are clear.

If you are engaged, your job is to fight the bogey as aggressively as possible, to force him into a predictable flight path, while keeping your partner informed of the bogey's height and speed, and of his manoeuvres, as well as the relative positions of the engaged aircraft.

If it comes to you to separate from the fight, the best manoeuvre is to turn hard towards the bogey's six o'clock, and orbit at about 3,000–5,000 yds. You then start back in when the bogey is on the far side of the fight, and should achieve a head-on position at about 2,500 yds. You can roll out in the bogey's six o'clock, using lead and lag to achieve the right range.

As an alternative, you might find yourself in a defensive two-against-one engagement. As a ground-attack pilot, universally known as a 'mud-mover', your job is to get to the target, attack it, and get back to base unscathed. You fly low, and you fly fast. If you can avoid it, you do not hang around engaging in complex dogfighting. Your duty is to see the enemy, counter his threat, and press on to the target.

Almost all flights to a ground target are flown in 'defensive battle' formation, with the two aircraft on parallel tracks, line abreast, at about 2,000 yds separation. It is not easy to judge the distance, but there are clues, and you will have already begun to learn about them at RAF Valley. In good light, for example, you can see your partner's canopy at 1,500 yds separation; at 2,000 yds his aircraft becomes not much more than a silhouette. The defensive battle formation offers the best compromise between control of the two aircraft, and the ability to provide mutual support. You can check relatively easily behind your partner's aircraft, and he behind yours. Whichever aircraft sees a bogey becomes the controlling aircraft, until the leader calls 'Tally' and assumes control.

Your reaction to a threat is to call the action and follow it up with information. The aim is to keep the bogey outside the 800-yd range. Usually, you can achieve this by turning the formation towards the bogey, increasing his angle-off, and forcing him to fly through. Your first call is 'Buster', a new term meaning full power, followed by a tac formation turn, or a counter. The usual result is that the bogey threatens No 1 aircraft, and turns with him. At 10 seconds into the fight he would need 10 g to keep following No 1, so has to break off, leaving him threatened by No 2 aircraft.

Sortie preparation includes the intelligence briefing, giving the position of surface-to-air missile and anti-aircraft artillery sites

(SAM and AAA), plus details of the FEBA (forward edge of battle area), enemy radar coverage, escape and SAR (search and rescue) cover, and anything known about the target, including, if you are lucky, photographs taken on earlier operations. A met briefing will already have produced details of the pressure, temperatures and winds in the target area. In early SAP exercises you might have over two hours to organise an attack from these details. Later, that time will be cut down. Squadron pilots expect to have no more than 20 minutes for their planning.

Mud-movers in training at a TWU use two maps for their operations. A low-level map shows the general area on a scale of 1:500,000. For the IP-to-target run, just as at RAF Valley, they have a 1:50,000 OS map overlaid with electricity supply cables. The exercise starts with a period of quiet study of the target information and the maps. Systematically, you begin to take into account the number of aircraft and the type of weapons you have at your disposal, the defences around the target and the time you will be exposed to them, your own safety separation over the target, and the terrain. From that you can decide the type of attack, whether level or pull up to dive bombing, the angle for the final run (tip-in) and the possibilities for a re-attack, which is almost never carried out in real-life combat.

You can work out how to attack the target, taking into account the effects of your weapons, the defences, your best view of the target, the position of the sun and the effect of the wind on your aim and on smoke, which might affect the aim of the second aircraft, any high ground beyond the target, and the availability of a good IP. A good IP is vital for a good target run, perhaps even the most important single element in the planning. It needs to be clear, to the point of being unique in its area; it should have vertical extent, so that you can see it from a distance and not just when you are on top of it; it must be between 5 nm and 15 nm from the target; it should be undefended, and not a hazard; and it should offer a good pre-IP point, or map change-over point, within 30 seconds of the target and not at too great an angle to turn on to the IP.

For dive bombing, an angle of 60 degrees is ideal, and that requires an apex 1.7 nm from the target, 1 nm on from the PUP, or pull-up point. Hawk trainee pilots and navigators carry a variety of plastic templates, except one for drawing this angle, but most have made one of their own, and can mark in the IP-to-target run from it. On that map you need to mark all the other relevant target information, notably the apex height, sight settings, the run-out plan, and the heading. Most pilots also ring the hazards in red, and any helpful ground features in appropriate colours — church towers in black, woods in green.

If your ATM calls for a time on target, you can begin to work back along the route from the target to the IP, and from there back along the low-level route. You have planned low-level navigation routes before, in the advanced flying training stage. Now you need to add some refinements, for flying in combat and in formation. What enemy defences are there likely to be? How much fuel should you allow for combat on the route? How much fuel will you need to recover to base, so how long can your route be? What cover can the terrain offer?

You will certainly need to avoid built-up areas; you can consider them defended, as well as noise-sensitive. And you should avoid areas likely to harbour combat air patrols (CAPs). If you can use the terrain to hide, but without flying along lines of communication, and if you can choose good clear vertical navigation features to make the navigation easy you will have an acceptable route.

Draw in your turning points, and each of the legs, and work out the magnetic headings. At these speeds you don't worry about the winds, so you can simply mark the headings under an arrowhead. Mark off the times, from your hack point, and write in the fuel figures, with Bingo and Chicken lines. Remember that you might be bounced, so some of your flying will be at higher than cruise power settings, and you will use a lot of fuel. Note the danger areas, and any specific areas to avoid by NOTAM, draw in headings, distances and frequences for diversion airfields. There is a recommendation at the TWU that says 'KISS' — Keep it simple, stupid. If you can assemble and assimilate all that information, and still regard it as simple, you are beginning to master the art of applied flying.

There will still be problems for the unwary, and as the instruction has it, somewhat illogically, always plan for the unexpected. The list of unexpected possibilities is endless: delayed take-off, bad weather *en route* or over the target area (it could make a dive-bombing attack impossible), excessive fuel consumption, loss of contact in cloud with your leader or wingman, bounce, aircraft unserviceability, and navigation errors. The art of navigation at this stage in the course seems to have become distilled into a straightforward principle somewhat divorced from the mathematical complications that kept you awake in the elementary and basic flying stages. Pick a big feature, and fly to it. Or, as they say in the notes, if you are perfectly on track all the way round then your lookout is not good enough.

In the search for simplicity, a number of rules of thumb can be applied to help the churning calculator in the brain, either in planning the SAP or in flight. At 420 knots the Hawk burns 22 kg/min of fuel; at full power 32 kg/min. At 250 knots, its optimum range speed, it burns 9 kg/min. Safety altitude, to which you pull up if the weather blocks you in, is 1,000 ft over the highest relevant obstacle, or 2,000 ft above if the terrain goes over 3,000 ft. Your indicated airspeed goes down by 5 knots for every 1,000 ft of height you gain. And if you increase or decrease your speed by 30 knots for two minutes, you can gain or lose 10 seconds.

Finally, the attack and the run out. The aim of the attack is to achieve the maximum time over the target for acquisition and accurate weapons delivery, while minimising the time you are exposed to enemy defences. You have to compromise. You also have to lead your formation on to the target in the most effective sequence, with the right spacing to ensure that none of them suffers from the damage effects of weapons dropped by an aircraft in front.

The best solution to these requirements starts with an approach in battle formation. If there are four aircraft, Nos 1 and 3 extend their separation to 2,500 yds line abreast, with Nos 2 and 4 swept 60 degrees 250 yds behind them. At the PUP No 2 drops back to 800 yds separation. In a pairs attack, at 10 seconds before the PUP No 2 checks the leader's six o'clock, flies a 4 g turn into line astern, and attacks the target with about 1,000 yds separation. After the attack, the aircraft need to regain cross-cover as quickly as possible, so the lead aircraft flies a 4 g turn away from and back on to track 2,000 yds off line, leaving the following aircraft in the correct position, back in defensive battle. It is a co-ordinated, elegant manoeuvre, and flown correctly will deal effectively with the target and leave the aircraft intact and unscathed.

All the navigation and tactical planning that go into preparing a SAP have been finished, the pilots and navigators have put on g-suits and life-vests, and collected their helmets from the equipment room. It is time for the attack briefing. Much of the flight will be covered by the Standard Operating Procedures, so the sortie leader will concentrate on items which are not standard. Among those, since the aim of the sortie is to attack and destroy a target, he will emphasise the attack itself. That still leaves a great deal to cover.

First, the air task message, so that everybody knows what they are aiming to do. Secondly, the intelligence, covering the general situation, radar cover and any knowledge of ground and air defences, the FLOT, and escape and evasion plans. The weather, with the latest base, *en route*, target area, and diversion details, with QNH values and winds.

The composition of the formation and 'domestic' details have to be made clear, though some of these are covered by SOPs, and only variations need to be specified. The plan to achieve cross-cover for the formation as soon as possible after take-off has to be established, as well as navigation details for the route.

Add recovery procedures, emergency procedures, including mission-abort circumstances, safety climb, radio frequencies and the fist-signalling codes, lost procedures, bird-strike responses, which can be considered the equivalent of battle damage, and which is a real hazard in the West Country flying area, and signals for low fuel states.

Brief on tactics, including how to report threats and how to avoid them, usually by staying low and avoiding unnecessary turns, and what to do if bounced. Since this is a target attack, the formation is briefed generally to get through to the target, and not indulge in air-to-air combat. The instruction is generally a 'Buster' call, to go to full power and outrun the threat, although it might prove advisable to turn to put the target head-on, run out at maximum speed to gain maximum separation, and return to track later.

Your formation needs to know precisely what it is attacking, so you will need to produce a target description, preferably with photographs. You have to specify the formation for the route and for the IP-to-target run, and give the time to pull up and the cross-over point. You also need to confirm the switch settings, which might be on the maps already but require this check, and the weapons selection. The attack profile will include the attack heading, the tip-in technique, the apex height, or the approximate height if you have planned a level attack, and hazards in the target area. With your drawing of the target, and the measurement that you have carefully calculated for its size, converted into mils, you can brief the acquisition and sighting details including the wind allowance. There remains the run-out manoeuvre, and your plan to regain the integrity of the formation, and the missed attack procedure. If you miss this one, do you have a second target to attack? Should you re-attack this one?

At the end, you can ask the formation any penetrating questions you like, to make sure that they have listened and understood your briefing. Then you can run a time check, and the formation can walk to the aircraft.

# 9

## The Complete SAP

At the end of the weapons course, the complete learning package is put together into a composite flight. You can be expected to demonstrate as wide a range of the skills as can be incorporated into a flight lasting up to an hour, which is as much as the fuel will allow at low level and with some full throttle manoeuvring. It is not so much a test. On this course the instructors have been watching you all along, and if you could not survive you would not have got this far. But the way you perform could determine the type of squadron you go on to. It depends on where your aptitudes lie, whether you would be better in a single-seat or two-seat environment, whether you are likely to perform best at high-level interception, low-level attack, or some other of the many roles of the modern air force, and on where the Royal Air Force currently has vacancies.

It is the complete Simulated Attack Profile.

We shall be No 2 aircraft in a two-ship formation. The sortie will start with a run north to the ranges at Pembrey, on the Welsh coast. The lead aircraft will fly a low-level attack and drop one bomb. We will carry out a 10-degree dive-bombing attack to drop our bomb. The middle phase of the sortie will be a run out over the Bristol Channel for some air combat manoeuvring, for as long as the fuel will allow. Then we shall drop down to fly an attack route at 250 ft round Devon, ending with a 'dry' dive-bombing attack against a specified target.

The sortie starts with a session of detailed planning in the SAP room, to prepare for the final phase of the operation. A young student navigator has been asked to select a target and supervise the route planning. He looks over the wall map of south-west England. It is studded with colour-coded pins for suitable targets of various kinds: bridges, water targets, electricity generation and supply buildings, and suitable airfields. To make the task reasonably easy, he settles on a large and distinctive target from the collection, a large dam on the Clatworthy reservoir on the eastern edge of Exmoor. Despite some highly acclaimed wartime exploits, dams would not be high-priority targets in future combat. They are difficult to breach, and when you have made a hole, you have not produced a great deal except a lot of white water.

Planning, just as at the advanced training stage, starts from the target and works backwards. We need photographs of the target from the intelligence file, and the relevant maps: the low-level map covering the whole route at 1:500,000, and the bigger OS map, overdrawn with electricity supply cables, at a scale of 1:50,000. Two maps for each aircrew member, eight maps in all. Close scrutiny of the photographs and maps together suggests that the most fruitful plan would be to attack the dam almost square on, approaching from the south and popping up to dive along the river valley from the south-eastern side. Spread the large-scale map out on the planning desk, and start drawing. Students carry a 60-degree-angled template, and with a small amount of manoeuvring it produces an excellent IP at the junction of the motorway and the main road. Mark in the triangular target marker, the square IP marker, and the IP run with the diving turn, just in the same pattern that we have practised at Pembrey.

Mark off the 10-second points along the route, up to the PUP where we shall climb to our apex to start the dive. The PUP is at 1 min 04 sec after the IP. Cast off and mark in the time at the target. So that the wingman and lead pilots both know where the other aircraft is, we mark the run for both on all the maps, with a suitable point where the wingman can turn and fall in line astern behind the leader. That looks like a good point to start to join, where the river curves away sharply to the right, at 42 seconds into the run, putting the wingman on line just beyond the electricity supply cables at 50 seconds.

Now calculate the height of the apex of the climb, just before the dive. At Pembrey the bombing circuit height is 2,500 ft, so here we need to add the height of ground at the base of the dam itself. From the contours we can read it off as 225 ft, so mark in the apex as 2,725 ft. Mark in the heading for the dive as 314 degrees. Now, somewhere close to the IP, write a summary of the essential information. It will include the heading for the run, 014 degrees; the time at the PUP, 1:04; the aim, Dive Dam; and a reference list which reads QDXB. Q is the QNH, the pressure setting for that area at the time of the attack; D is the depression used for calibrating the bomb sight; X is the crosswind component; and B is a reminder to dial in B on the sight for a bomb run. A telephone call to the met office gives the predicted pressure, temperature, and wind vector for the eastern edge of Exmoor at our arrival time, and we can fill those in. The pressure will be 1001. The crosswind component, calculated by the simple sine rule method, is 20 knots from the left. And the depression, read off from the appropriate graph on the wall of the SAP room, for the local temperature and pressure is 116. That figure will be dialled in on the bomb sight on the last leg of the route, just before the IP.

The remaining part of the navigation planning is the low-level route. We choose a route that will take us in over land at Hartland Point, on the north Devon coast, and on a heading of 172 degrees to Launceston, turning at 3 min 30 sec on to a heading of 132 degrees to arrive at Tavistock at 5:00 min. A leg of 2 min 10 sec on 100 degrees will give us a turn at Ashburton on to 020, to fly to Crediton at 9 min 40 sec into the flight. A leg from Crediton to arrive at Cullompton at 11:45 on 076 will lead to a final turn on to 019, to reach the IP at 12:00 min into the flight precisely. We mark in the routes, minute intervals along it, and circles with times around the turning points. The headings are marked clearly with arrowheads alongside each leg. At the IP the clock starts again and continues through the run out from the target on a heading of 309, turning at the lighthouse at 4:15 on to 270 for the run home.

By this time we shall probably have run out of available fuel, on this busy sortie, so we shall organise the return to base according to the fuel state. In any case, we mark in a big chicken fuel circle, with fuel required at various points. We have to land with 350 kg remaining. We also need to mark in the NOTAMs, particularly the two mink farms near the Cornish coast which we must not overfly.

With the low-level and target maps complete and folded carefully to make a cardboard-stiff pad, there is a third major item in the planning. For the type of bomb run flown in the Hawk, we need to calculate the bomb-aiming picture. For that, the lead pilot has to perform some interesting intelligence interpretation work. We have to measure the width of the dam. Only then can we estimate how many mils it will subtend when we are at the 1,667-yd position. The dam occupies about 0.5 cm on the map. That is not entirely an accurate calculation, so we pore over the photograph for more reliable indications. Cars are quite good as a reference, with the family saloon averaging 14–15 ft. There is a camping van in a field, but it is some way behind the dam, so its scale cannot be absolutely trusted. The sluice gates on the dam itself could be an indication, if we assumed from intelligence that they were 10 m wide. Weighing all these indicators, we estimate that the effective part of the dam, between the ridges of the hills on either side, is 110 m. That is the picture that we shall use to gauge our 'uncage' point.

We shall be attacking the dam square on, so we do not need to make an amendment for the apparent width. All we need to do is calculate how many milliradians the dam subtends at our uncage distance of 5,000 ft, or 1,667 yds. Then we can draw our 'uncage-sight' picture on an overhead projector briefing slide. We can also draw the picture as we expect to see it when the sight tracks along the ground to the pickle point. Collect together the maps, photographs, and briefing slides, dump the discarded portions of all maps in the rubbish bin to keep the SAP planning room tidy, and go off to the briefing room.

A good, crisp, clear, comprehensive briefing is one indication that a student may be a good leader and a capable pilot. He is expected to carry out the briefing in a professional manner. It includes full details of the sortie, aircraft, aims, and the activity. A briefing student will throw random questions at the other pilots and navigators, regardless of their status as his instructors, and they are expected to answer correctly.

'What is the signal for an oil problem, Flight Lieutenant Blank?'

'Er, clenched fist, then four fingers.' The Flight Lieutenant makes the signal.

'No, it's five fingers.' It is a familiar trap, and the Flight Lieutenant has fallen into it. The mnemonic is HEFOE – H for Hydraulics (one finger), E for Electrics (two fingers), F Fuel, O Oxygen, E Engine. Oil comes under Engine, with five fingers. The O is for Oxygen, not for Oil.

Perhaps most important, the briefing gives the chance for the pilots to study together the details of the route, especially the IP-to-target run. The IP is a very clear one, the junction of the main road with the motorway. Running on 014 from that is the wood at 14 seconds, and the village with the church at 24 seconds; the church should be clearly visible. There is the long wood where we cross the river at 40 seconds. At 48 seconds we shall cross the electricity cables.

On our side of the run we have the canal on our left for the first 30 seconds, then the river on our right. Where the river runs away to the right, with the church on our left, we turn hard left to fall in line astern behind the leader.

'The clear feature in the distance, with the 200-ft tower on top of the 1,447-ft hill, should be visible. There is the funnel feature of the main road coming in from the left, and we cross it at one minute. The pull-up-point is just as we start to come abreast of the village of Wiveliscombe.'

We have drawn over or marked in a variety of colours the main features – woods, cables, churches, towers. We are looking for vertical features that will stand out at a distance, and long funnel features that will lead us along our course. At Chivenor the students are encouraged to read the map as though it were tilted away from them, and even to tilt it and look horizontally along its face, to visualise the route not vertically from overhead, since at 420 knots that is largely irrelevant, but as it looks coming up ahead of them from their viewpoint at 250 ft.

We brief on three 'Bingo' times, when we will call a fuel check, and on our weapons load for the first phase of the sortie.

It has been said over and over again, and applies just as much at the TWU, that the key to a successful flight is thorough preparation. When we believe we have thoroughly prepared our sortie, we go out to the aircraft. Ours is Hawk Tango, with the 151 Squadron white diagonal cross on its blue background.

Strapping in produces the usual mixture of emotions – impatience at the laborious process tinged with excited antici-pation at the prospects of the flight. Fighter pilots still feel it, every time. First, the rudder pedals. Release them, push them forwards to a comfortable leg length, and lock them in position. Maps at the side. Helmet in the well formed by the open canopy. Pass the leg-restraint straps through the rings on your garters and lock the ends home into their respective recesses. Pull the central locking strap up through the middle, pass the leg straps over, and then the shoulder straps, thread them through their network of holes, and lock the buckles home. Tighten the leg straps, then the blue straps, then the top shoulder straps. A lever to your side goes forwards to let you lean forwards freely, backwards to lock your shoulders in place during the flight. Click home your personal equipment connector. Roll on your helmet, and clip the mask into place. The other end of the mask tube goes into your life-vest connector. A helper clicks home your radio plug, and you can talk to the instructor. You adjust the intercom and radio volume on your right. You have a switch on your left for 100 per cent oxygen, and a yellow striped switch on the left of your seat to pull for emergency oxygen. You are now totally plugged in and strapped into the aeroplane. At least one visor down and eyes shut just in case the explosive cord should detonate and shower you with shards of perspex, and the canopy comes over and locks into place.

There are two safety pins whose job is to prevent the canopy release and ejection seat from working. Take them out of their housings and clip them into the stowage points provided. As the briefing video says, you are now sitting on a loaded gun.

Test the g-suit by pressing the button. It squeezes you sharply across the abdomen and down the legs. It works. You are going to need it.

For several minutes the checks go on, and the start-up procedure develops, until we wave away the chocks and roll forwards, check the brakes with a lurch, and swing round to taxi out behind our lead aircraft in Oscar.

The formation take-off is familiar, although the rotation less brisk than at RAF Valley, with the bomb-containing canister under the wing. Over the coast we break belly-up to each other, and fly out into defensive battle formation, with 2,000 yds between us, flying north over the glistening grey sea. The coast of Wales is clear ahead, including two small islands on the Swansea peninsula: first Worms Head, then Spanish Island. From there it is a straight clear run to the Pembrey range. We fall into fighting wing formation, to watch the fall of the leader's bomb. He will make a straight run to the target for a level bombing FRA, or first run approach. There is no preparation, no reconnaissance or rehearsal. Just line up with the two markers, fly over them and the bomb target is ahead. Ahead and just below us he pickles his bomb. It falls away, a tiny speck below his aircraft.

The standard Royal Air Force practice bomb is about 18 in. long and weighs 3 kg. It should produce an explosion of brightly coloured smoke. The range officers call the bomb as 5 ft left of target. There is some dispute as to whether it was a UXB – an unexploded bomb – since we saw no explosion. The range officer was satisfied with it. We pull round into the circuit and climb rapidly to 2,000 ft for our approach. It will be a dive-bombing run.

There is a set circuit for the Pembrey ranges, designed to keep the aircraft away from sensitive areas and out of the adjoining danger area. Fly inside the railway line, to avoid the village of Kidwelly, and towards the chicken huts. When the target comes into your nine o'clock make a hard level turn, overbanking slightly to bring the pipper up directly under the target. After pickling the bomb, pull 5 g for the recovery, turn downwind, carry out your checks, and turn in for another run if you have planned to. The circuit is flown at 350 knots.

Downwind, after the leader's level run, we calculate the crosswind component using the sine rule, from the wind provided for us by the range officer. It resolves into 20 knots from the left. Dial it in. We already have the depression dialled in, and the weapons sight set to B for bombing. The target is coming up on the left. We are at 2,000 ft. Turn hard left now, overbanking, and ease the stick forward to fly down the flight path. Watch the picture as the target grows in the bomb-sight circle. We know that the target will occupy 30 mils at the correct 'uncage' point for dive-bombing. It is growing, growing, growing, so uncage . . . *now*. You flick open the flap on the control stick with your thumb. The pipper and circular sight drop away out of sight. Now fly the bug to keep the aircraft on the flight path. Bug, bug, bug. Lock your arms. Don't be tempted to drop the nose towards the target. The pipper in its circle appears again below the target and begins to track across the ground, running up the sight glass. Watch for it approaching the target, and just before it crosses the centre of the target, pickle the bomb . . . *now*. Pull 5 g directly for the recovery, and at 2,000 ft turn downwind to assess our performance. The range officer reports us just left of target. We feel we had been given a wrong wind, but we are satisfied with our effort.

Back into battle formation to climb out over the Bristol Channel for air combat manoeuvres. We shall first carry out the ciné-weave. It is an introduction to the art, an opportunity for the student to experience, in a predictable sequence, the technique of keeping the gunsight pipper on a moving target. The leader, who is the tow aircraft for this sequence, dives down to 5,000 ft. The Hawk gains or discards height so freely he suddenly becomes an almost invisible spot, light grey above the grey sea. I follow him down, lose him in a small cloud, recover visual contact, and stay just above him as he begins to circle. When 420 knots shows on the airspeed indicator, I fall in line astern of him. Through the gunsight he fills 15 mils on the pipper. His range is between 250 and 350 yds. I have to keep it in those margins. Wait until the sun is in our seven o'clock, then call, 'Com . . . mence.' The exercise begins on the second syllable. We both count for three seconds, maintaining the formation . . . one thousand and one, one thousand and two, one thousand and three . . . then he banks hard over left in a 4 g turn.

I follow, pulling hard to bring the pipper on to his cockpit. Too much, and it pulls right through him. Relax the g, and he swings back through my gunsight. I need more delicate movements, but there is no time for delicacy. I have forgotten to count.

After precisely 12 seconds in the 4 g level turn he rolls off the bank to 30 degrees, but holds on the g. If I had been counting, or had been more familiar with the aircraft or the sequence, I might have been ready for him. His change of bank with the same g sends his nose up and he climbs into a barrel roll. I roll off my own bank, and try to follow him with the pipper. He stays somewhere in the middle portion of the gunsight, but the pipper refuses to stay on him. Too much wavering, pull a bit more, and more. We have tried to be too delicate and have lost the g. Behind him the sky has changed to sea, and he is charging down the hill. The end of the barrel roll is coming up, and he is about to roll right. Follow him over . . . *Now.* Too late, and the ciné-weave ends before we can bring the pipper to bear.

Straight into a second try. Apply full power and climb level to 1,500 ft above our 5,000-ft datum. Roll towards him, and pull 2 g to keep him in the frame. Speed 430 knots, and we should be catching him. With the pipper on him he should be 15 mils in the gunsight at the correct range. That looks about right. So call 'Com . . . mence.' One, two, three, roll left, and pull. Not quite enough, so pull some more, too much again. Roll off, and up we go. Add some power to maintain the range in the climb. Aim to stay at 300 yds, which requires a 34 mil picture. He wavers, seemingly flying wildly, but I am experienced enough to know who it is who is flying inaccurately. Down the other side of the roll, ease off the power or we shall overtake. Try to keep the pipper on him. Then roll . . . *right*. And call 'Out!' Switch off the ciné.

Check the fuel. There is time for a short bout of air combat manoeuvring. We fly level and start circling. In a turning fight against a similar aircraft this would be stalemate, with neither aircraft able to get into a shooting position on the other's tail. We can only win by tightening the turn. Let's try a high yo-yo. Climbing will slow us down, so we can achieve a tighter turn radius. If we then loop into a descent, at the top of the arc we shall have an extra 1 g, as gravity aids us to start coming down. With our slower speed and extra g we should be able to pull a tighter turn than him. So pull up, pull up, pull up, and bank in a high wingover. It sends us outside the original circle, but suddenly we are turning tight at the top of the climb and coming down again, miraculously at a greatly reduced angle off. One more of those and we could achieve a firing position.

That took some more fuel, and we still have to fly the SAP. So we switch back to battle formation and head for the coast. There is Devon, and the headland at Hartland Point is clear. Map up. Dive to the coast, hack the watch, and tuck right in at 250 ft. Advance the throttle to give 420 knots, and trim. The aircraft wants to climb. Trim it nose down slightly. At these speeds it is not easy to achieve a sensitive trim. After the tranquillity of high level, the countryside flashes by below at incomprehensible speed. There is a lot to do. We have to fly, accurately and smoothly. We have to navigate, and this is a six-leg sortie to our IP. We have to keep the formation, in defensive battle, which means a continual eye on the leader, 2,000 yds away and easily lost to sight, sometimes against the sky, sometimes below the horizon against the brown landscape. And we have to keep a check on the sky behind him. Officially, this is not a bounced sortie, which means that nobody from the squadron has been detailed to intercept us on our track. But not everybody knows that, and nobody else knows that we are a student on a training sortie, so we would be fair game for any aircraft looking to embarrass us, and even for a pilot from one of the aggressor squadrons who patrol the skies to promote a high level of awareness among NATO pilots and force them to practise and refine their evasion techniques. In any case, it is essential to maintain the lookout, if only as practice for the bounced sorties to come.

'Go right. Go right.' I have been straying off my heading of 179 for the first leg, and my instructor has spotted the mink farm up ahead. How he distinguishes the mink farm from other buildings dotted about the landscape is a mystery, but he guides us round it. The landscape here is a flat, grey-green, with small fields and occasional woods, typical agricultural England. Anxious to anticipate, I glance at the map to try to spot the next heading. I dare not look away for too long, with the ground only 250 ft below. It becomes a struggle. 'Watch your speed.' I have the ground, the map, the leader, and the speed to watch. I am not even sure that the map is the right way up, and I know that I need at least three hands to keep the sortie going: one for the control stick with the trim under the thumb; one for the throttle, and one to keep the map in front of me and the correct way up. And I need three pairs of eyes, to keep the aircraft flying safely ahead, to keep a lookout for the leader and for any bounce aircraft behind him, and to keep an eye on the map.

Remember not to over-navigate. Think vertically, pick a point, and fly to it. The work cycle should help to sort out the confusion. I decide on priorities, and elect to keep the aircraft safe. It is no use flying it into the ground at the right place on the sortie.

Launceston is coming up ahead, and we shall turn here. All turns are assisted turns, and we are going to turn left on to 132 degrees. Watch the leader. And keep an eye out ahead. Suddenly he banks left sharply towards us, and the Hawk is silhouetted against the sky. Our job is to help him round this turn, watching his six o'clock while he watches ours. The technique is to turn towards him, initially away from our next heading. So bank right . . . *now*. He flashes towards us and overhead, and now we turn left, hard over, to come out on our new heading. Now he is over there to the left of us. We have been able, in theory, to watch each other's six o'clock in the turn, producing a shorter period of vulnerability than if we had simply turned in formation. That is the assisted turn.

Check the watch. The next leg is a short one, with a turn ahead at Tavistock on to 100 degrees. That should be at five minutes into the flight. We are skirting the southern edge of Dartmoor, aiming for a cable pylon, and there he goes. The leader begins his turn towards us. We turn towards him and he comes over and on to the other side. Another assisted turn.

'Watch your height.' Am I too high or too low? Too high, and a gentle push on the stick brings us down to a suspiciously low height. The instructor seems satisfied. Trim out the aircraft, and follow the contours. We are over the hilly Dartmoor landscape now. Somewhere nearby should be the prison at Princeton, but we pass without my seeing it. Keep an eye on the leader. Check his six o'clock. Look around. Watch the speed. Add a touch of power to keep up to 420 knots. We are getting a bit close to him. Ashburton comes up and we have to turn on to 020. I have almost lost track of the navigation and opted to leave it to the instructor. We start the turn, and I begin to get used to the balletic movement of the changeover, and a bit more confident in banking the aircraft.

It is time to change the sight to the bombing mode. Down below the control column I have to reset three knobs. Refer to the attack map, which lies tucked away at the side of the cockpit coaming. It gives the depression and crosswind. Dialling them in distracts my attention from the task of flying the aircraft. At this height that could bring disaster. Do one thing at a time. First dial in the crosswind with the knob on the left. While I look at it I let the aircraft drift up away from the ground. Go back down. This is a high-threat environment and we need to stay low to take advantage of the cover. Dial in the depression on the right. Take the aircraft down to 250 ft again. Look for the leader. Look out behind the leader. Watch the heading. Pause, and fly the aircraft. Give yourself time. Down off Dartmoor and Crediton is coming up. Just time to change the gunsight mode to B, so that is set up. The next heading will be 076, and the leader is turning now. Turn towards him, and swing away when he goes out of sight, then pick him up on the other side, and settle on to the new heading. Watch the height. Watch the speed.

It is busy, difficult to stay ahead of the aircraft.

We are skirting the edge of Exmoor now. On high ground ahead there is a mast, like a totem pole decorated with white concave dishes. It is on a ridge. Pull up before we get to the ridge. Don't get too close to it. We pass almost below the top of the mast, and suddenly are exposed high above the ground on the other side of the ridge. It is bad flying. I should have anticipated the ridge more, and lifted the nose before we crossed it. Then I would have been able to cross it while descending, to regain our 250-ft height as soon as possible after crossing the ridge.

Cullompton coming up, and it is time for another turn, closing, over and under, and out on the new heading, 019. Check fuel. Check speed. A gentle squeeze on the throttle brings it back up to 420 knots, and I am beginning to feel for the aircraft, and to feel part of it, rather than pushing its controls around as though it were a mere machine. And there is the IP, the motorway.

Everything is happening in rapid succession on this last part of the sortie. The leader is over on the left. Hack the watch. I nearly forgot. Bump, bump, bump – stop, reset, restart. Even that takes seconds and we are into our run. Ditch the low-level map and out with the half-mil map.

'Very accurate flying now, please. We are in a high-threat environment around the target.' The instructor is calm and reassuring. They always are.

I try to read off the main features on the map. He can do all this and talk at the same time.

'There is the motorway with the canal coming up on our left. We are crossing the cables. Look ahead for the river going off to the right, with more cables ahead. Now hard left turn, in behind the leader. There we are crossing the main road, and that is the village of Wiveliscombe over on the right. One minute and a few seconds gone so pull up now.'

We pull straight up with g coming on, and there, over on the left, is the bright water of the reservoir, sickle shaped, with the dark mass of the dam standing out against it, a straight edge across the top, and merging into the banks of deep green countryside at either end.

Overbank now, and pull out in a 10-degree dive. We should have been at 2,725 ft, but I was too concerned with the target to check the height. The bombsight pipper appears over the black background. I try to remember the 30-mil picture, which will put us on the correct flight path, and sight line. That looks about right, a small dam behind a big circle. Uncage now, and the pipper falls away. Now fly the bug, bug, bug, and the bombsight begins to track up the picture towards the base of the dam, and there is the pipper, so pickle ... *now* – and pull up to 5 g to clear the dangerous high ground on the other side of the reservoir, and back up to 2,000 ft.

The fuel state is now becoming critical. We have planned a run out along the northern coast, but the leader calls for a direct route home, and contacts Chivenor, requesting priority on the grounds of fuel state. On the track home Chivenor becomes visual at about 10 miles. We reduce the speed to 360 knots and I fly formation on the leader. Not too close. Just enough to keep station in fighting wing, to the right and rear of him. Even that is not easy. You begin to get low, so you pull the nose up and advance the throttle. That brings you level, but you now have too much throttle, so you start to catch him up at an alarming rate, and risk overtaking him. Ease back the throttle, but the Hawk is a slippery aircraft, so you need a touch of airbrake. That slows you too much, so you need more throttle, and you begin to catch up again.

Ahead a Hercules appears at our height, growing bigger by the second. The instructor takes control and pulls right, then waggles his wings to indicate visual contact as we pass wingtip to wingtip at what must be a closing speed of 700 mph. That brings us behind the leader, and I take control again, following him in for a run in and break. The circuit is left so we arrive at 360 knots and about 300 ft, on the right side of the runway. Just past the threshold he breaks left. Count one, and two, and three and break left, pulling up to 1,000 ft and easing back the throttle to idle. The aircraft arrives downwind still climbing, and gets to 1,200 ft before I notice and ease it back down, and continue to bank round.

'Aim to roll out at 130 knots, and arrive at the threshold at 118 knots.'

I tip in for the finals turn and at the 400-ft point roll the wings level and fly the aircraft down towards the piano keys, point it and gently manipulate the throttle. Then the threshold comes up so check nose up slightly, close the throttle, pause, and suddenly the aircraft arrives with a firm and definite contact on its main wheels, so relax the stick and watch the nose tip neatly forward to bring the nose wheel down. A firm but reasonable landing.

The entire sortie – take-off to landing – has taken 45 minutes. It may not have been entirely representative of a pilot's day in a war, but a hot dive-bombing run, followed by an air combat manoeuvre, followed by a simulated attack profile culminating in a pop-up and dive against a dam, includes many of the elements that the student has to learn. If he adds to that evidence of his ability to perform satisfactorily with a 50 mm gun under the aircraft, and can carry out the evasion techniques to prevent a bounce aircraft from getting into a firing position in his six o'clock, he will pass out from the Tactical Weapons Unit with selection for one of the Operational Conversion Units (OCUs). There he will learn to operate the aircraft he might well ultimately fly in combat, and he will take a further major step forward in his flying and operational skills.

# 10

# Viffing and Pressups

The Harrier cockpit is tight and compact, but high off the ground. Ahead is the runway at RAF Wittering, all 9,000 ft of it. You will need hardly any of it. You are cleared to take off, so advance the throttle to check the engine, and ease it back again. All is ready, so advance the throttle to full power once more, brakes off, and wait for the surge of acceleration. This aircraft accelerates like no other. It is more than a kick in the back. It is a thrust forward that tries to take your helmet off the back of your head. The first time you fly, it takes you by surprise, almost to the extent that you forget what you are supposed to be doing. But concentrate. This is your first take-off in a Harrier, and you have this abundance of thrust to play with. You have carefully calculated the correct take-off speed, taking into account the weight of the aircraft, its weapons load, the fuel, and the temperature and pressure of the day. Now you simply need to watch for 120 knots coming up on the airspeed indicator. There it is – 120 knots – so hand across on to the nozzle lever down next to the throttle on the left side, and pull it smartly back to the STOL (short take-off & landing) stop. That movement changes the direction of thrust from directly aft to 55 degrees downwards, and the aircraft becomes airborne like a leaping deer. Once you are comfortably airborne, you can advance the nozzle lever again to vector the thrust fully aft, then select gear and flaps up. The Harrier accelerates smoothly away. You have used only a few yards of the runway.

Some pilots claim that the Harrier, among all the aircraft types available, is the one that attracts the best of the pilots.

It is a single-seat fighter, so the workload is greater than in an aircraft with a two-man crew. It has the well-known ability to perform a short – and, if required, vertical – take-off, and a short or vertical landing. In the Royal Air Force the pilot almost always performs a short rolling landing. In the Royal Navy it is more often vertical.

The versatility which that technology offers calls for special flying abilities – greater even than those needed in orthodox fighter aircraft. A Harrier squadron is also a coveted posting because of the kind of work that the Harrier does. Because of its versatility, it is a front-line aircraft, used most frequently in close support of ground troops. It might be assigned to low-level bombing runs, to reconnaissance missions looking for targets of opportunity, to air superiority tasks, or to interception, as the Royal Navy mainly uses it.

Where other aircraft offer one kind of flying, the Harrier calls for a range of skills, and in return offers a wide variety of activity. A great many pilots want to fly the Harrier. Only the best are given the chance. Those who are selected pack their bags in Wales or Devon, at the end of the TWU course, and travel eastwards to 223 Operational Conversion Unit, RAF Wittering, in the East Midlands. RAF Wittering is proud of its title: 'The Home of the Harrier'.

There, after the customary introduction to the aircraft in ground school, the Harrier pilot immediately leaves RAF Wittering for a temporary assignment at RAF Shawbury, to learn something about flying in helicopters. Harriers are expensive to buy and to fly, and as the student will soon discover, they are sensitive to handle, so the student must learn the craft of hovering in something less expensive and less unforgiving. The Gazelle helicopter gives them that skill.

From that point on, there is a special range of skills related to Harrier flying, and they amount to a new aerial art form. You have taken off, flown the first half of a standard circuit, and you are downwind. Make the calls, but instead of turning finals from the end of the downwind leg for a landing on the runway, you are going to land on one of the short strips that lead off the taxiways and main runway at Wittering. You have about a hundred metres to play with. The Harrier will handle it in a short landing. But you need to handle the controls carefully.

So, tip in from finals and line up the aircraft, then ease back the nozzle control to 60 degrees, and adjust the attitude. The aircraft begins to slow down. Hand across to the throttle, and adjust it. If you sneak a glance to the side you will get an idea of how slowly you are travelling across the ground. Watch the airspeed indicator, and look for 50 knots. Keep the aircraft coming down with throttle control, and gently adjust the attitude with the control column. Slowly, gently, the Harrier approaches the threshold of this abbreviated landing area. Keep it coming down, down, down, and as the ground comes close, you need to get down on to it. If you do not land firmly, you will be close enough to be exposed to ground effect from the jets' hot gas, and the reaction from the thrust on the ground can throw you out of balance. So close the throttle, and the aircraft lands with a very firm thump, and rolls gently forwards. You are down.

The instructor seems quite satisfied: 'You can see how easily the aircraft can operate from a short stretch of motorway close to a front line. Turn the aircraft to taxi back to the end of this short strip.'

So, call your intentions, turn the aircraft, and taxi back. Carry out the checks, turn it round, and make the final check of the engine with a run up to full power and back.

The take-off is the same as you have carried out before, but this time you do not have the comforting sight of 9,000 ft of runway in front of you. Your take-off area runs out frighteningly close, on to the grass in the centre of the field. It could be treetops, or a bridge, or a building, close to the front line. But you have flown the take-off before, so advance the throttle to full power, and this time add water injection for more power. Again you feel the surge of acceleration. At 50 knots pull the nozzle control smartly back to the 50-degree position, and up she goes. It is almost like levitation. Advance the throttle control to nozzles aft, and out she flies to join the circuit again. When you have mastered the art of taking off and landing on short strips, you need to learn the techniques for grass, if only to prove that the aircraft needs no runway at all.

'If you would like to take us along the taxiway to the point where the grass starts to look worn and brown, you can carry out a take-off and landing from the grass area.'

Again, you carry out the familiar checks, then turn hard round and taxi on to the grass, leaving the runway at a 45-degree angle so that you don't put both wheels on to the softer area at the same time. The Harrier bobbles and shakes on the uneven surface. It is an experience you haven't seen since your early days at the local flying club. Most fighter pilots have put grass taxiing long behind them.

Now keep going. The last thing you want to do is stop, and give the heavy aircraft the chance to sink in to an uncertain surface. Run it across to the area that looks distinctly singed, where you know other Harriers have been before, and turn it to line up parallel to the orthodox concrete runway. Now straight up to full power, and at 65 knots again ease the nozzle control back. It lifts perfectly easily off the grass. Fly a circuit as tight as you like, and tip in to line up again with the same grass area. You have carried out the strip landing already, so all you need to do is repeat it. Gear down, flaps down, and nozzles down to slow the aircraft. Now control the rate of descent with the throttle, and keep the wings level and the nose in the right place, using the control column. Just keep it coming down at a sharp angle of descent. Use only slight adjustments, and make sure you monitor the airspeed. You do not want to go below 50 knots of forward speed, or you might bury the wheels in the grass. Keep it coming down, then when you are almost there and risk going into ground effect, pull the power, and get it firmly down – *wham* – and rolling forwards. Flaps up again, and taxi off the grass area.

You have learned the techniques for conventional take-off and landing, and for short rolling take-off and landing. Now for the ultimate test of the Harrier's versatility.

'Taxi round to the concrete pad at Bravo East, and we will try some pressups and hovering.'

When you last hovered an aircraft, in the helicopter preparation phase at RAF Shawbury, it was in an aircraft with a rotary wing – whirring blades overhead that looked as if they were designed to make the aircraft hover. The Harrier equally is designed to hover; it just does not look like it or feel like it. This is going to be a novel experience.

Bravo East is one of the small square pads dotted around the Wittering airfield, just clear of the runways and taxiways. Half-way along each side is a small marker. Line up with any two markers, and you are in the centre of the pad. They are your reference points. The aim of the lesson is pressups: lift the aircraft off the pad, take it up to 100 ft, hover there for as long as it takes to make sure you can control the aircraft in the hover, then let it down for a vertical landing.

First, the familiar checks again. Then make sure the nozzle control lever is fully aft to give vertical thrust, and apply full power. The Harrier lifts as if by magic. But you are going to need all the co-ordination at your disposal now. The slightest touch of departure from the vertical, and the four lines of thrust will send you lurching away from the centre of the pad, either sideways or forwards. As it rises, the aircraft tries to tilt, so work to hold it with the stick. At least that has got rid of the list. Now, at 100 ft, ease off the power, so that the aircraft stops flying upwards. It loses its jetborne lift, and promptly begins to descend, because you took off too much power. Apply a touch more, and up it goes again.

You get the feeling your instructor is just waiting for everything to go totally wrong before he takes control. But you have more than a couple of hundred hours of flying behind you now, and you were judged to have the aptitude for Harrier flying, so he can afford to trust you for a while longer.

There are still problems. In the time you were concentrating on getting the height right, the aircraft has drifted, and it is turning as well. You need to get it back to the centre of the pad. So first stop it turning, with a touch of rudder. Not bad. Now inch it forwards towards the position where the lines from the markers intersect. Advance the control column a little, just with pressure, and the nose dips, the thrust goes slightly rearwards, and the aircraft advances.

So far so good. But now, with the thrust not quite vertical, you have lost some of the jet lift, and the aircraft has descended. Advance the throttle. That starts it lifting, and because the thrust is towards the rear, the aircraft gathers forward speed. You can feel the sweat gathering on your brow. Pull back the stick to stop the inevitable advance., You have already overshot the centre of the pad. And the fuel is rapidly running out. As the stick comes back the nose comes up and, with the thrust now forwards, the aircraft starts to drift to the rear. Stick forwards, and before you know it you have started a gentle rocking motion that gets worse as you try to correct it.

'I have control.' The firm voice of your instructor tells you that you have not done well. 'Just very gentle movements,' he advises, 'and centralise everything as soon as you begin to get the controls right. You have control.'

You still need to go forwards, so apply just the slightest pressure, and then return the stick to the centre. Just a touch, then another, and gently, like a benign elephant in a circus, the Harrier nudges its way forwards. Give it a touch of rudder to turn its nose towards the heading you want. And as you apply the slightest touch of control with the column, at the same time add the merest hint of thrust with the throttle. Play the two against each other, in perfect balance, and you will stay totally steady over the spot you have selected. Your flying is rusty, since it is some time since you hovered the helicopter, but with a gentle touch, and a little finesse, you are managing to iron out the embarrassing lurches.

'Now turn it on to a heading of Zero Three Zero, and let down for a vertical landing.'

He wants you to display your control of the rudder pedals. So just a touch of right rudder, then centralise, then another touch and off again, and remember to play the right hand on the control column and the left hand on the throttle. Now the landing. All you need to do is ease off the throttle, and the Harrier will start to go down. Just gently now. But the secret is to work the hands independently. While the left hand eases off the throttle, the right hand must keep control of the stick, not allowing any deviation from the steady thrust from the nozzles, in beautiful equilibrium.

This is the most dangerous part of the exercise. Lose too much power and the Harrier will sink like a stone, with disastrous consequences to the pilot and instructor and to the aircraft. Lose control of the thrust vector through the control column and the aircraft will be descending out of balance, and you risk breaking out of the outriggers.

The secret lies in restraint. Just a margin at a time, just the gentlest of touches, and the aircraft will begin to descend. Now reapply most of that touch of power which you took off, and the descent will be checked, but will continue. Hold it like that. Keep it balanced with the control column, and hold the nose steady with the pedals. Both of your hands, and your feet, have to work independently, and with absolute co-ordination. Now you are coming into ground effect, and risking foreign object ingestion if there is any debris on the pad, as well as unwelcome thrust from the recirculating gas, so you need to complete the landing quickly. Throttle closed, hold the column central, and thump ... the

Harrier is down. You are not sure that you really had control, but you have completed the sortie.

'Now taxi back to the apron, and we'll have a debrief.'

You have already seen that the Harrier's vectored thrust gives it the advantage of being able to operate in a wide range of environments away from concrete runways. But those advantages are available not just during take-off and landing. Do you recall air combat manoeuvring, from your days at the TWU? You will be able to use some of that extraordinary versatility in air combat. And the Harrier conversion unit is the place where you can develop your skills.

Line up with your partner aircraft for the familiar formation take-off, conventional style. Checks completed, power on, brakes off, and roll. At this stage in the course you take for granted these skills which once seemed so advanced and testing. Clean up the gear and flaps and fly in unerring formation through the cloud layer.

You are about to engage in the ultimate joust, aerial combat that is breathtakingly fast, prodigally expensive and so bewilderingly unpredictable that it demands not only total concentration and split-second judgement but calls on all your reserves of professional skill as a pilot.

You are in formation with another Harrier, flying out from Wittering eastwards to the play area over East Anglia. You break through the cloud at 7,000 ft, into the glittering blue. The cloud surface is an infinite expanse of perfect white, like a pure tufted carpet on which to enjoy the game. You have started a combat like this before, but not previously in the Harrier, and not at this level of competence. And for the first time you have a head-up display to help you.

So, on the command from the formation leader, split and separate out to five miles distance. The last you see of the other Harrier is his planform, peeling away from you, until you pick him up again, a speck in the distance, hard to spot at first, but clear black against the white of the cloud, perfectly visible once you know where to look for him, tiny, and menacing as a black widow spider.

You turn and fly in towards each other, right wing to right wing, building up speed so that he flashes by at a closing speed of over 800 knots.

So turn. Wings over and pull g. Hard. Your head is twisted to the side and your helmet tucked into the corner of the cockpit, with your eyes swivelled to peer through the edge of your visor, looking for him. If he has turned the opposite way to you, you will pick him up almost instantly. He is not there, so he has turned away from you. You have no choice now but to keep pulling and turning. You do have a choice about whether to go high or low. Trust your instincts. You feel you would like to go high. So ease back on the stick. Not too much, or you will sacrifice performance. Controlled aggression is what you need, with the emphasis on the control. Just pull it to the light buffet. And stop worrying about your neck aching. It comes with the job.

Then suddenly there he is in the corner of the cockpit. Pulling round with you. If you go on like this you could spend all day circling each other and never come to a conclusion. So call, 'Knock it off' and fly out for another approach. Turn, and back in again. Pass, and turn. This time, turn high straight away. Pull, and twist your head round. And try to follow the other aircraft. You have him in sight. He is going low, so pull down towards him, over the top with a huge wingover. You have followed him over the top, and you are speeding down the other side. All you see is the aircraft you are chasing, and the bubbly white line between the cloud horizon and the blue sky. But that line is not behaving rationally. It is wheeling incomprehensibly in front of the cockpit, now horizontal, now gone altogether and replaced by a plain of deep blue, now reappearing, but no longer horizontal, just wheeling and moving down the canopy, then disappearing and being replaced by a new expanse of white. You have stopped orienting yourself according to the real world, and now you can refer only to the other aircraft. It is a mistake. Next time you will have to keep a clear idea of which way up you are or you will not be able to take advantage of the pull of gravity – the familiar egg. Again, you have embarked on a stalemate turn, but this time going round as if round the rim of a cartwheel spinning virtually on its edge. So call again, 'Knock it off.'

You need to learn how to give yourself a bit of an edge. You need to introduce the idea of viffing. To viff is to vector your thrust in forward flight – VIFF. The American operators of the Harrier, the US Marines, call it thrust vectoring.

So let's spend a lesson having a look at viffing. In the Falklands war the Harrier pilots came out with a reputation for having an uncanny ability to let enemy pilots get into their six o'clock, then direct the nozzles down so that they slowed down and climbed at the same time, while the offending enemy pilot flew past them, and they came out on his tail. The flaw in the argument is that if you ever let an enemy pilot get on your tail, you are dead. You might, as a last desperate resort, try the manoeuvre, but you ought to make sure that you say your prayers at the same time.

Just to show what would be possible if you did want to try thrust-vectoring with the enemy on your tail, fly level just above the clouds. Advance the throttle fully, and watch the speed climb up above 450 knots. The clouds, still looking as impenetrable as a snowfield, are flashing along beneath the aircraft. So ease back the nozzle lever gradually to 60 degrees. Keep an eye on the airspeed, and keep the aircraft in the correct attitude with the control column. The clouds begin to slow down in their headlong flight below us, gently at first, then quite dramatically. As the aircraft slows, it feels as though we are tethered on a giant strand of elastic.

Spend a moment contemplating where another aircraft would be now if it did not have that capacity to vector its thrust. It would be somewhere out there in front of you, or more probably pulling a high-g turn to get away from you. You might be able to turn round for a snap shot, but you have just about given up all your energy, and are becoming increasingly vulnerable. Let's complete the manoeuvre anyway. The clouds are still slowing down. It is like riding a fully controllable magic carpet, and in seconds the Harrier slows to a complete halt, and hovers above the clouds, at over 7,000 ft, trembling slightly, like an eager thoroughbred waiting for its next instruction. It is extraordinary.

In a fight, the real value of viffing is slightly different.

'Let's fly a maximum rate turn, and see what we can achieve.'

Nozzles aft again, build up the speed, and set up the aircraft for a high-speed high-g horizontal turn. Roll it on to a wing, pull, and wind the nose round the horizon. Track the nose along the cloud line, to get a measure of the turn rate. Now pull the nozzle control smartly back to vector the thrust downwards. The effect is to speed up quite sharply the rate at which the nose runs round the horizon. But not for too long. Nozzles rearwards again after a couple of seconds, or you will run out of forward momentum, and lose the energy that is your most precious asset. Now imagine what that capability would give you in a turning fight, if you could just pull that little extra in a tight turn to give you a missile-firing position or a gunshot.

'OK. Level out and gain speed, and now fly a big wing-over.'

You pull up into a steep climb, and keep pulling, and turn to the right. It is just like the top of a high yo-yo. You fly the Harrier up, and over, looking up under your eyebrows, and pulling the aircraft through the vertical until the light buffet starts to burble and the nose winds rapidly round the sky and starts to come down towards the horizon. Now draw back the nozzle lever to vector the thrust downwards, or in this almost inverted attitude upwards towards infinity. The instant effect is to pull the nose sharply down into the turn. You have changed the direction of the flight, far more radically than you could ever do with aileron and elevator control alone. It is sensational. Advance the nozzle control again, and you are going downhill into what would be the centre of a one-against-one fight, but with the advantage of a tighter turn, and with your speed and energy virtually intact. So pull out into level flight, and start to appreciate the advantage you will enjoy in your next encounter.

'May I try that again?'

'Sure. Go ahead.'

There is a subtle change in your relationship. Your instructor has become your guru. The pedantic formalities of rank, and to some extent of the passing of control between pilot and instructor, have been dropped, and replaced by the easy informalities of mutual respect.

So, full power, and pull up. At this stage, the g forces, and the hugging of the g-suit, go almost unnoticed. There is nothing but bright sky ahead of you. Bend your neck back to look out of the top of the canopy, and watch for the appearance of the upside down world of the cloud horizon. Get your brain into order to orient yourself. You are looping, and turning, and about to start flying down the other side of the turn, so nozzle lever back, and there it is, the instantly sharpened increase in the turn rate. And there you are flying down the hill on the opposite heading to your entry.

Now you need another Harrier with which to fly some combat. The arrangements are made with an available instructor in the operations room. He is asked to fly without viffing, to simulate dissimilar combat with an orthodox aircraft.

Again the start of the fight is the same. Fly out to the play area in formation, split to five miles, establish visual contact, turn, and fly towards each other for a high-speed pass. Then pull, and roll, and you are going upwards into the great blue, with the light buffet burbling off the Harrier's wings. Somewhere behind you he is turning and working to come into your six o'clock. You are flying up into the sun, so down with the sun visor for protection and for better vision. Keep your head swivelled to look for him, and there he is, etched in black against the white clouds below. The sun tracks out to your left, and you come up to the top of the great arc of your turn, and over. Using the viffing technique ease back the nozzle lever, and the turn rate increases momentarily. As you start down the other side of the turn, ease the lever forwards again, and the speed builds up, with the other aircraft swinging beneath you down below and across the right. It is almost impossible to read what he is doing, but he is now only half a cockpit to the right of you, so you appear to be winning the turning contest. He begins to swing up above you. The only choice is to follow him round, so at the bottom of the turn pull up to 6 g and start to climb again. He is up in the overhead now, and you are following him up into the climb, as though the pair of you are pinned to the edges of a great wheel. He is making for the sun, and suddenly he becomes lost to view, somewhere in the great ball of dazzling yellow overhead. There is only one rule in the world of combat training. If you go into the other guy's sun, stay predictable. As long as he does not reverse his turn, you should stay well away from him, until he comes out of the sun a few seconds later. There he is, perfectly silhouetted in planform against the blue, himself a dark metalic blue-grey, in the familiar shape of the Harrier. He is not far off your nose now. In the head-up display, the aiming device for the Sidewinder missile is tracking on to him. It is a small diamond, and once you get that on to the enemy aircraft, you can launch the missile. Its infra-red seeker-head will do the rest. Uncover the missile launch trigger.

You are following him up the hill, and giving up speed, so let's roll slightly, and let's try viffing. Ease the nozzle back, and the nose comes rapidly towards him, and there is the aiming point tracking across his fuselage, so squeeze the missile trigger. He is dead. Call: 'Knock it off.'

You are going again for a second fight. This time you are looking for a gunshot. The bogey flashes by again, and you roll and pull left, with the g inflating the suit, and the arms straining to stay on the controls. This time, he has flown an opposite turn, and you are coming round towards each other. In a fight like this, with either aircraft free to manoeuvre in three dimensions, and to point in any of nearly 130,000 different degrees of direction, the development of the fight is totally unpredictable. The choice is to keep turning towards each other, and going into a stalemate, or for one aircraft or both to change direction. The usual course is for both aircraft to change direction and end up flying cockpit to cockpit in another variation of the stalemate.

You both change direction, and fly parallel to each other, climbing towards the sun. The sight for the gunshot is a small circle of outward pointing lines, looking as pretty and innocent as a snowflake.

The other pilot is an experienced instructor, and at this stage in the learning process knows when a student needs to be given a chance. To avoid another futile crossover, he turns away from the circle. Pulling round to follow him, you lose all sense of orientation. Are you upside down, or pointing down, or flying round? The line of the horizon is tracking across the cockpit, and blue is becoming white. The other aircraft is growing slightly smaller, and moving down through the canopy windscreen. The g is still pulling at the arms and legs, and then begins to relax. You are coming down the hill, and pointing at the earth, and tracking towards the bogey, and gradually, as you turn tighter than him, he comes steadily on to the corner of the screen of the head-up display. A touch of the nozzles brings him even closer to the pretty little snowflake, and after a couple of seconds it starts to track up towards his fuse-lage. He ought to start to jink at any moment now, to spoil your gunshot, but you have the snowflake on him and you are pulling it through him. Squeeze the trigger. It is time to claim a kill.

There is much more to learn about the skills of air combat. You have to understand the art of air defence, intercepting incoming aircraft. You have to put your air combat knowledge into practice for one-against-two, two-against-two, and other multiple engagements. You have to study and understand the constantly developing performance of the weapons which you carry. And you have to study and understand the performance of the aircraft against which you might find yourself flying in a war, and the performance of the weapons which they carry.

Air combat, like all interesting professions, is one in which you never stop learning and developing. When you finish your course at the operational conversions unit, you are assigned to your squadron. It is now months, and rapidly becoming years, since you embarked on your early lessons in the basics of flying, but you are still not fully qualified as a fighter pilot. You are a junior pilot in your squadron, and your squadron leader has a considerable responsibility to bring you up to the standard where he is satisfied that you can perform at the level he requires, should your squadron go to war.

In those early stages on the squadron, you will at first be deemed only Limited Combat Ready – LCR in NATO terminology. It is the term by which NATO counts you as one of its reserve assets. It might still be months before you have enough air experience and advanced training to be regarded as a fully capable pilot. At any stage in those early months, indeed at any stage in your career, you can be taken out of service as being below the standard required for the job. But you will not be the squadron's most junior pilot for long. Other pilots are coming along, nearing the end of the long hard road which is the fighter pilot's training system. They, like you, have suffered the elation and the disappointment. They have found some of the course easy and some of it almost incomprehensible. They have survived the many opportunities to be chopped, and are about to join their squadrons, just as other pilots who have years of experience are moving out of the front line and taking up other assignments.

Your aim, at this early stage in your front-line career, is to play a full part in the fighting life of the squadron. To do that you will have to convince your commander, and his superiors, that you would be capable of acquitting yourself well should the squadron go to war, and for that you will have to demonstrate that you can lead other pilots in a formation in the event of hostilities. When you can do that, you will at last be counted not as one of NATO's reserve assets, but as one of its front-line assets. You will also have

191

a new designation, to confirm that you have passed out of the ranks of raw trainees, and have achieved the first rank of mastery in your profession.

You will be deemed Combat Ready.

# Epilogue

When I started researching this book, the forces of NATO and the Warsaw Pact glared at each other across Europe; Communism was the accepted system of government throughout the Eastern bloc; and Germany was in two parts, with an impassable wall across the partitioned city of Berlin.

In the course of 1989 and 1990 that picture changed. The wall came down; democracy asserted itself throughout Eastern Europe; and there was a welcome thaw in the political climate between East and West. In short, the Cold War ended.

In the United Kingdom, the government ordered a review of the nation's defence needs, and the result was a substantial reduction in the Royal Air Force's presence in Germany, the removal from service of some squadrons of older aircraft, and the 'mothballing' of some Tornado aircraft.

The expected consequence might have been a drastic cut in the requirement for combat pilots. There has been no such cut. In mid-1990 events in the Middle East demonstrated that the improvement in international relations is far from universal, and that the requirement for capable, highly trained, well-equipped armed forces is as great as ever. For the foreseeable future, we shall still need combat aircraft, and pilots to fly them.

Those pilots, moreover, will need to be of higher and higher quality. As the technology of military aircraft advances, the profession will call for increasing standards of technical competence, physical ability, and judgement, and will make ever greater demands on recruits in all the disciplines of military aviation.

The message to young people today is simple. A career in military aviation is far from irrelevant. It is as challenging, as demanding, as fulfilling, as worthwhile, and even as essential, as it ever was.

# Glossary

| | |
|---|---|
| A A A | Anti-aircraft artillery |
| A C M | Air combat manoeuvring |
| A S I | Air speed indicator |
| Bingo | A call to a formation leader to confirm that fuel is adequate to complete a sortie |
| C C I P | Continuously Computed Impact Point |
| Chicken fuel | A calculation of the minimum fuel required to return to base from any point in a sortie |
| C F I | Chief flying instructor |
| D H | Direct Hit |
| F E B A | Forward Edge of Battle Area |
| F L O T | Forward Line of Own Troops |
| F P B | Flight Path Bug |
| I M C | Instrument Meteorological Conditions |
| I P | Initial Point |
| L F C | Low Flying Chart |
| Navex | Navigation exercise |
| O C U | Operational Conversion Unit |
| Pickle | Press the button to release a bomb |
| P U P | Pull-up-point |
| Q F E | The altimeter setting for the airfield and circuit area |
| Q F I | Qualified flying instructor |
| Q G H | The magnetic bearing to an airfield |
| Q N H | The regional altimeter setting used away from the airfield |
| S A M | Surface-to-air missile |

| SAP | Simulated attack profile |
| SOP | Standard operation procedure |
| TWU | Tactical Weapons Unit |
| VMC | Visual meteorological conditions |